VIKING

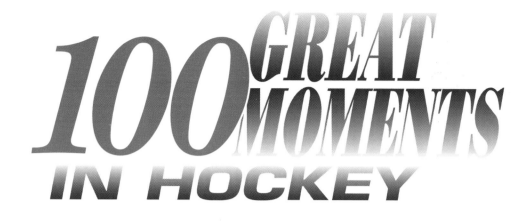

100 GREAT MOMENTS IN HOCKEY

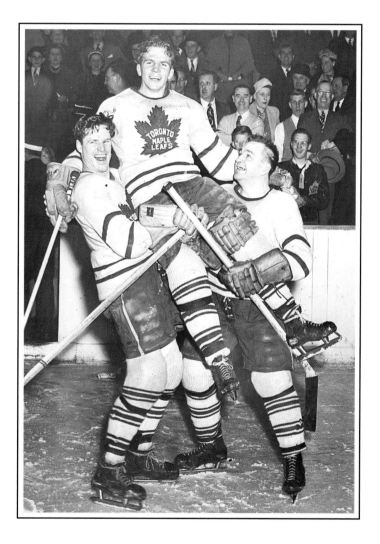

BRIAN KENDALL
Introduction by Ron MacLean

VIKING

VIKING
Published by the Penguin Group
Penguin Books Canada Ltd, 10 Alcorn Avenue, Toronto, Ontario, Canada M4V 3B2
Penguin Books Ltd, 27 Wrights Lane, London W8 5TZ, England
Viking Penguin, a division of Penguin Books USA Inc., 375 Hudson Street, New York, New York 10014, U.S.A.
Penguin Books Australia Ltd, Ringwood, Victoria, Australia
Penguin Books (NZ) Ltd, 182-190 Wairau Road, Auckland 10, New Zealand

Penguin Books Ltd, Registered Offices: Harmondsworth, Middlesex, England

First published 1994

10 9 8 7 6 5 4 3 2 1

Printed and bound in Italy on acid neutral paper.

Canadian Cataloguing in Publication Data

   Kendall, Brian
   One hundred great moments in hockey

   ISBN 0-670-85798-X

   1. Hockey - Pictorial works. I. Title.

   GV847.K45 1994   796.962'022'2   C94-930777-7

For Jack and Thelma Kendall,
the best hockey parents a boy ever had;
and Sharon McAuley,
my linemate for life.

Introduction

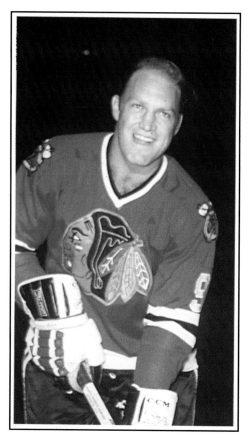

A few summers ago a hockey player of some renown was participating in a charity golf tournament in Moncton, New Brunswick. As the man was trudging up the 16th fairway, the young radio news reporter he was partnered with mentioned how the game of hockey had changed. With all the ease with which oldtimers sink two foot putts, the player told the reporter that there were still 4 corners, 3 zones, 2 nets and 1 puck. The math, you see, is the same. It's the myth that is hard to master.

In this beautiful collection of great hockey pictures, the world's fastest sport stands still. Brian Kendall has captured a century and enabled us to hold it, stare at it and understand it. The mind races over frozen images. Games are played on sheets of ice that are entirely smooth save for the goosebumps.

I have spent a good deal of my professional career trying to figure out my broadcasting colleague, Don Cherry. Don is roughly twice my age and two times my wage. He is famous for his explosive opinions. In the ample time we spend together during the Stanley Cup playoffs I often probe his past to try and determine his blueprint.

On a flight from Edmonton to Chicago in 1992 the clue I had been searching out was revealed in a hockey picture. Cherry and I were seated across the aisle from each other in business class. I was reading the formal newspaper, he was perusing the tabloid. At 39,000 feet I got to the bottom of what makes Don tick. He pulled away his reading glasses, leaned over the armrest toward me and pointed out a picture of two players in the throes of a fight. He explained that out of all the things he missed about playing hockey, the most emptiness resulted over having grown too old to engage in fisticuffs. We gazed at that picture and reminisced all the way to O'Hare.

It's not that I'm so crazy about black eyes. I see the inside of an eyelid as a canvass. When we absorb a photo and close our eyes we begin to paint. All that the painting requires is framework. And that frame is the story that accompanies each of these pictures. When given a backdrop such as the time remaining in the game, or the importance of the game, the images suddenly have context and texture.

From Lester Patrick, the coach who turned goaltender in a legendary overtime game, to Bobby Orr's horizontal climb to the top, the faces and surroundings provide enough material to make a 200-page read an endless pleasure. Furthermore, since these are not staged photos, there is truth in the dreams published here.

My boyhood hero was Jacques Plante. Turofsky's snapshot of Plante, wearing his newfangled mask, shows a man driven to try anything to win. *100 Great Moments in Hockey* is a collection of excellence that uncovers the myths created by those 4 corners, 3 zones, 2 nets and 1 puck.

Ron MacLean

Ron MacLean

Author's foreword

Writing this book provided both considerable joy and just a little frustration for a longtime hockey fan like myself.

The joy, of course, was in the opportunity to relive so many of the greatest moments in the game's history. As I researched and then wrote about the heroics of such famous figures as Rocket Richard, King Clancy and Howie Morenz, the past came alive for me as it never had before. I now *almost* feel that I was there when Richard scored his five goals in a playoff match against Toronto, and when Lester Patrick came off the bench to backstop the New York Rangers to victory.

My personal memories of the events recounted here kick in around 1960 when I was eight years old and, like most Canadian boys, completely absorbed by the sport. Several times every season my father would take me to games at Maple Leaf Gardens. Our tickets, which had been in the Kendall family since the building opened in 1931, were up in nosebleed country — the first row of the Greys. But before making the long climb up the stairs, my dad and I would always stop at one of the entrances near ice level so that I could clearly see the faces of my heroes as they warmed up.

Locating the photography to best bring Howe, Richard, Hull, Orr, Gretzky and the game's other legends sharply into focus at the most critical moments of their careers was the toughest challenge presented by this book. A great deal of time and effort was spent in searching out the pictures seen here. Some of them, such as the wonderful old sepia-tinted shot of the young Foster Hewitt, are valuable originals. While the publishers and I are indebted to all our suppliers, special thanks must go to Phil Pritchard and Craig Campbell of the Hockey Hall of Fame for their assistance and generosity.

The frustration I mentioned earlier came from trying to decide which 100 moments would make the final cut. Many were so obvious that they simply couldn't be overlooked. Others were more obscure, which I think makes their telling all the more compelling.

I'm sure readers will be as moved as I was by the bitter recollections of Willie O'Ree, the first black to play in the NHL. I also think they'll chuckle right along with "Sudden Death" Mel Hill as he reflects on the curse of his famous nickname.

As work progressed on the book, I found myself thinking more and more about those boyhood visits to Maple Leaf Gardens with my dad. Most of the games he took me to involved the Detroit Red Wings. Unlike all of my friends who lived and died with the Maple Leafs, I was a Wing fan and a devout worshipper of the god named Gordie Howe. I can still remember the thrill I got from standing there during the pregame skate and staring close up at quite possibly the greatest player who ever lived.

Young boys before me felt the same way about Howie Morenz, Milt Schmidt and Rocket Richard. Today's kids have heroes named Gretzky, Lemieux and Gilmour. Over the years the names and even the game keeps changing. But in our memories and on these pages, our heroes and their greatest moments are ours to keep.

Brian Kendall

"This is what every kid dreams of, scoring the winning goal in a Stanley Cup overtime final. Wow, I can't find words to express what I feel."

- Boston's Bobby Orr in 1970

Heroes are not ordinary men

Lester Patrick and the birth of a legend

> *"If you need a goalkeeper, why the hell doesn't Lester play?"*
>
> *- Montreal coach*

Hockey's most famous tale, retold countless times and often embellished in the fashion of Babe Ruth's "Called Shot" of baseball lore, tells how silver-haired New York Ranger coach and manager Lester Patrick donned the goalie pads and sparked his team to a Stanley Cup championship.

In the second period of a scoreless second game of the Cup finals, the Rangers, who had dropped the opener of the best-of-five series to the Montreal Maroons, lost the services of their ace goalie, Lorne Chabot, who went out with an eye injury.

Teams didn't carry spare goaltenders in those days, so Patrick asked the Maroons for permission to replace Chabot with Alex Connell, an outstanding goaltender for the Ottawa Senators who happened to be at the Montreal Forum that night.

"If you need a goalkeeper, why the hell doesn't Lester play?" came the reply from the Maroons bench.

"I will, by God, I will!" an angry Patrick retorted. He was 44 years old, and had played goal a couple of times before, but never in such a tense situation.

Playing low on the ice, often on his hands and knees, Patrick repelled attack after attack by the Maroons. Early in the third period, the Rangers scored to take the lead. But after Patrick had been forced to make two more brilliant saves, the Maroons finally beat him to tie the score and send the game into overtime.

The Maroons kept up the pressure. Patrick sprawled on the ice to make two stops before Frank Boucher of the Rangers stole the puck and scored the winning goal.

Patrick was paraded around the rink on the shoulders of his mates.

"I stopped only six or seven really hard shots," the hockey legend, who became known as the Silver Fox, said modestly after the game. "My teammates saved the old man with their backchecking."

Patrick didn't want to tempt fate again. With hastily acquired goaltender Joe Miller in goal for the remainder of the series, the Rangers went on to win their first Stanley Cup.

Patrick later recalled how he "donned Chabot's uniform, skates, and what have you, and everything fit perfectly except the skates. I took care of that by putting on an extra pair of socks."

Smythe buys Maple Leafs a King-sized heart

October 10, 1930

Three years after assuming control of the Toronto Maple Leafs, managing director Conn Smythe felt confident that his team was headed towards lasting success. The Kid Line of Joe Primeau, Busher Jackson and Charlie Conacher was one of the most lethal forward combinations in the league. Other standouts included Hap Day, Red Horner and Ace Bailey.

But there was one player Smythe felt he needed to turn the Leafs into Stanley Cup champions. Frank "King" Clancy was a flamboyant, rushing defenceman for the Ottawa Senators, whose 40 points the previous season had set a record for rearguards. He was exactly the type of win-at-all-costs leader Smythe was looking for — and he was available.

The financially strapped Senators were willing to part with their 27-year-old captain for the then unheard of price of $35,000. Smythe thought Clancy was worth every penny, but the team's board of directors refused to go higher than $25,000.

Then fate in the unlikely shape of a race horse named Rare Jewel, an unpromising nag owned by Smythe, intervened to bring Clancy to Toronto. One day Smythe placed a bet on his horse more out of loyalty than any serious hope that she would win. But Rare Jewel, after being given half a flask of brandy by her trainer, ran the race of her life to finish first. Smythe's bets paid off at staggering odds. As he counted out his winnings of over $10,000, he remembered thinking, "Now we can buy Clancy. Now we are going to win the Stanley Cup."

"What do you want to be paid?" asked Smythe when his new star reported for duty. "Anything you say," replied Clancy, who loved the game so much that he would have played for free.

"I paid a fortune for a heart, the gamest heart in pro hockey," Smythe said of the little Irishman who led the Leafs to a Stanley Cup championship in 1932. "Clancy brought character, courage and devotion to the Toronto Maple Leafs."

Clancy was exactly the type of win-at-all-costs leader Smythe was looking for.

Clancy proved to be worth every penny of the $35,000 Smythe paid for him. He led Toronto to the Stanley Cup in 1932, and to two regular-season titles before he retired in 1936. In the photo at right, Clancy is welcomed to the Maple Leafs by coach Art Duncan.

Richard 5, Toronto 1

"They used to put Bob Davidson out to check me every game," Montreal's Rocket Richard said of the tactics used against him by the Toronto Maple Leafs. "Sometimes he stayed so close to me that I got angry, and that night I guess I took it out on him — and the puck."

Richard's spectacular five-goal performance in the second game of the 1944 semi-final equalled a single-game playoff record established by Newsy Lalonde in 1919, and served notice that hockey had acquired an almost unstoppable new star.

Playing alongside Toe Blake and Elmer Lach on what had come to be known as "the Punch Line," the third-year veteran scored 32 goals — 23 of them in the last 22 games of the season — in his first big season. The Canadiens finished in first place, and then met Toronto in the opening round of the playoffs.

Defensive specialist Bob Davidson threw a blanket over Richard in the opener as the Leafs won 3–1. "I remember going up to their goalie Paul Bibeault near the end of the third period and telling him things would be different in the next game," Richard said.

There was no scoring in the opening period at the Montreal Forum, but Richard finally broke loose and scored on a pass from Blake at 1:48 of the second frame. Blake and Lach set him up again just 17 seconds later. Before the period was over he'd added another, and the crowd gave him a standing ovation as he headed for the dressing room.

Exactly one minute into the third period, Richard golfed a rolling puck past Bibeault for his fourth goal. His record-tying fifth came at 8:54, when he swept the puck into the net after falling in the Toronto goalmouth.

To the delight of the crowd, Richard was named the first, second and third star in Montreal's 5–1 victory.

"The funny thing is that when we beat the Leafs 11–0 three games later, I only scored two goals," remembered Richard, who sparked the Canadiens to their first Stanley Cup victory in 13 years. For the 23-year-old Rocket, two goals had already become an off night.

Richard was named the first, second and third star in Montreal's victory.

The Rocket displayed an intensity that could be frightening to behold — especially for goaltenders. "When he hit that blue line and he saw an opening, his eyes would light up like a pinball machine," said Glenn Hall. "I only had six or seven shots on goal all game," Richard recalled of his five-goal playoff performance, "and every goal was scored in a different way."

9

Barilko took a pass from Meeker and charged across the Montreal blue line.

Bill Barilko's overtime memorial

Toronto defenceman Bill Barilko watches as his shot eludes Canadiens goaltender Gerry McNeil for the goal that won the Stanley Cup. Looking on are Montreal's Rocket Richard and Butch Bouchard (3). Barilko died weeks later in an airplane crash.

Even if tragedy hadn't soon made the moment even more vivid, Bill Barilko's overtime Cup winner against the Montreal Canadiens would still rank as perhaps the most dramatic goal in playoff history.

For the first and still only time in post-season play, every game of the Stanley Cup final was decided in overtime. The Toronto Maple Leafs won the opener on a goal by Sid Smith. Three nights later Montreal's Rocket Richard evened the series. Then Ted Kennedy put Toronto back in front. And Toronto drew to within one game of clinching when Harry Watson beat Hab goaltender Gerry McNeil at 5:15 of extra play in the fourth game at the Montreal Forum.

The fifth and concluding match would forever belong to Barilko, a brash, handsome 24-year-old defenceman from Timmins, Ontario, whose battling and bashing on the Leafs blue line induced terror in the hearts of enemy forwards. Canadiens boss Frank Selke said he hated Barilko so much he wanted him on his team.

With Montreal ahead 2–1 late in the third period, a few in the full house at Maple Leafs Gardens had already started for the exits. Then, with just 37 seconds remaining, Tod Sloan pushed a rebound past McNeil to send the game into overtime and the patrons rushing back to their seats.

Barilko's chance came less than three minutes into extra play. Never one to hesitate when opportunity presented itself, he took a pass from Howie Meeker and charged across the Montreal blue line, propelling himself through the air as he released a shot that sailed over a crouching McNeil into the net.

Hoisted on the shoulders of his mates, the beaming, waving hero savoured the greatest moment of his life.

"We just out-Irished them," joked Toronto's managing director Conn Smythe after heartily congratulating Barilko in the dressing room. Then Smythe was handed a telegram of congratulations — signed by a Father H. Murphy. "See what I mean?" he said. "Pure Irish luck."

A few weeks later Bill Barilko's luck ran out. Returning from a fly-in fishing trip to James Bay, he and the pilot died when their plane crashed into a forest north of Timmins.

The courtship of Jean Beliveau

October 3, 1953

"All I did was open the Forum vault and say, 'Help yourself, Jean,'" Montreal Canadiens managing director Frank Selke quipped to the press after finally securing the services of Jean Beliveau, already a hockey legend at the age of 22.

For two years Beliveau rejected every overture from the increasingly impatient Canadiens. His junior contemporaries Dickie Moore and Bernie Geoffrion had already become stars with the big team. But Beliveau chose to retain his amateur status and remain in Quebec City, moving up to the Aces of the semi-pro Quebec Senior League for the 1952–53 season.

Beliveau said he didn't want to disappoint his fans. On the strength of his enormous popularity, the Aces often attracted crowds of 15,000 at the Colisée and filled the Forum when they visited Montreal. Next to Rocket Richard, Beliveau was the most popular player in the province.

There was actually little incentive for him to move on. Although officially still an amateur, Beliveau was being paid as much as most NHL stars.

No one doubted that he would be an instant success with the Canadiens. "The NHL certainly must know by now that my boy rates only with Gordie Howe and Rocket Richard in their league," his coach, Punch Imlach, told the press.

Under intense pressure from their fans to sign the young star, the Canadiens finally felt they could wait no longer. In a dramatic move, they bought the entire Quebec Senior League and turned it professional.

Although Beliveau now had little choice but to join the Canadiens, he continued to hold out until Selke agreed to a $20,000 signing bonus and a five-year pact worth more than $100,000. The deal made Beliveau one of the two or three best-paid players in the game.

Standing behind Beliveau as he signed the contract in Selke's office was Canadiens coach Dick Irvin, who, perhaps foreseeing the years of Montreal glory to come, made a V for Victory sign at the gathered reporters.

For two years Beliveau rejected every overture from the Canadiens.

Next to Rocket Richard, the Quebec Aces sensation was the most popular player in Quebec. Beliveau had shone in two brief trials with the Canadiens, scoring six goals in five NHL games.

Hockey's forgotten pioneer

> *"There were always racial remarks made to me by other players."*
>
> *- Willie O'Ree*

More than a decade after the fanfare that surrounded Jackie Robinson's integration of major league baseball, Willie O'Ree became the first black to play in the NHL — and hardly anyone noticed.

"There wasn't much of a big thing made of it in the papers the next day," recalled O'Ree, who was 22 when he was called up from the minors by Boston for a game in Montreal. "My teammates were even kind of surprised about that. They said, 'Willie, this is history you're making.'"

Playing left wing on a line with Don McKenney and Jerry Toppazzini, O'Ree made his debut at 3:10 of the first period. He also played in the Bruins next game, then was sent back down to the minors.

O'Ree returned to the Bruins at the start of the 1960–61 season and saw action in 43 games, scoring four goals with ten assists. Traded to the talent-laden Canadiens in the off season, he never again played in the NHL.

The native of Fredericton, New Brunswick, reflected on a career marred by unrelenting racial abuse. "Teammates, by and large, accepted me," he said. "But there were always racial remarks made to me by other players after the whistles."

He was often goaded into fights. "Somebody was always saying something about my colour. I felt it was my duty to stand up for myself."

Most difficult to accept were the constant taunts of the fans, because there was no way to fight back. Spectators would sometimes throw black hats onto the ice to ridicule him.

After 25 years in pro hockey, O'Ree retired in 1980. The most he'd ever been paid for a season's work was $17,000.

O'Ree said he often wondered how different his career might have been if only he'd been a little younger when the NHL expanded in 1967–68, and if fans and opponents had been able to forget the colour of his skin.

"No matter how hard I played or how fast I skated, people just kept making references to my colour," said the man known as hockey's Jackie Robinson. "I wanted dearly to be just another hockey player, but I knew I couldn't."

O'Ree finished his career with the San Diego Hawks of the Pacific Coast Hockey League in 1980. In recent years he has received an honorary degree from Saint Thomas University in Fredericton, and was the subject of a documentary.

*"I won't go back in
without the mask."*

- Jacques Plante

16

Man in the mask

As a doctor worked to close an ugly seven-stitch gash under his nose, Jacques Plante confronted coach Toe Blake in the Canadiens dressing room at Madison Square Garden. "I won't go back in without the mask," said the goaltender stubbornly. Teams didn't carry spare goalies in those days, so a reluctant Blake was forced to give in. Plante returned to the ice wearing the plastic face mask that until now he'd only dared to use in practice.

The four-time Vezina Trophy winner wasn't breaking entirely new ground. In 1930, Montreal Maroons goalie Clint Benedict had briefly worn a crude leather mask to protect a broken nose. That experiment ended when the mask fell off and Benedict broke his nose again.

It was left to the innovative Plante (the first goalie to routinely roam from the net) to lead goaltenders into a new era of full facial protection. After suffering two broken cheekbones, four broken noses and a fractured skull, Plante decided enough was enough and, in partnership with a Montreal businessman, developed a plastic mask moulded to fit his face.

Toe Blake adamantly refused to allow Plante to use the mask in a game, convinced it would reduce his goaltender's field of vision. Then came the night in New York when, early in the game, Ranger star Andy Bathgate released a shot that Plante, who was screened on the play, never saw. The puck smashed into his face. Dripping blood across the ice, Plante headed to the dressing room and his confrontation with Blake.

Fortunately, Plante played superbly when he returned as the Canadiens won 3–1. "Blake told me to wear the mask until my injury healed," the goaltender remembered. "So in Detroit one night, I had to take it off again. We lost. Blake came to me and said that I had a chance to win a fifth straight Vezina Trophy that year, and that if the mask would help, 'do what you want.' So I put it back on."

Plante did indeed win another Vezina that year and went on to win two more during his Hall-of-Fame career. No one ever asked him to take the mask off again.

At left, a battered Jacques Plante poses for photographers the night he first wore his mask in NHL action. In the top photo, Plante makes a glove save on a drive by Toronto's Bob Pulford.

"I guess I must have been excited," Howe said of his historic marker. *"I went to jump and fell on my knees."*

Gordie Howe overtakes the Rocket

November 10, 1963

"I knew it was in when I let it go."

- Gordie Howe

"I'm glad it's over," a weary Gordie Howe said. "Now I can start enjoying life again."

The pressure on Howe to overtake Rocket Richard's career mark of 544 goals had been almost unbearable since the start of the 1963–64 season. In the two weeks since he'd tied the record in a game at the Detroit Olympia against Richard's former Montreal teammates, Howe had been unusually tentative around the net. The great Gordie had just four goals to his credit well into the second month of the season.

Now the Wings were back home at the Olympia, once again facing the Canadiens. Late in the second period Howe was sent out to help kill a penalty. Teammate Billy McNeill raced down the ice after taking a pass from Howe deep in Red Wing territory. Inside the Montreal blue line, McNeill passed the puck back to Howe, who snapped a wrist shot toward Montreal netminder Charlie Hodge from 25 feet out. Hodge tried to hug the goalpost to his left, then banged his stick in frustration when he realized the puck was behind him.

"I knew it was in when I let it go," said Howe, whose wrist shot was once timed at 114.2 miles per hour and was famous for its accuracy.

Bedlam broke out in the Olympia as the capacity crowd of 15,027 stood cheering for almost ten minutes. After the game, which the Wings won 3–0, Howe accepted a painted portrait of himself from Jean Beliveau on behalf of the Montreal team.

Rocket Richard was quick to offer his congratulations. "I knew he would get it," Richard said in Montreal. "He's a great player. How about that, scoring both the 544th and 545th goals against my old team."

The shutout king

When Detroit's Terry Sawchuk had tied George Hainsworth's all-time shutout record back on November 10, 1963, his achievement had gone almost unnoticed. Detroit teammate Gordie Howe stole the goaltender's thunder that night by breaking Rocket Richard's career goal-scoring mark of 544.

But Sawchuk stood alone in the spotlight when he blanked the Canadiens 2–0 at the Montreal Forum to record the 95th regular-season shutout of his career. The 14-year veteran made 36 saves, many of them "bordering on sheer thievery" according to a local paper.

A high-strung, often moody man, Sawchuk told reporters that during the game he hadn't been thinking about the record, which Hainsworth had set while playing for the Montreal Canadiens and Toronto Maple Leafs from 1926 to 1937. "I didn't give a darn," he said. "The win was more important."

Urged on by the press, he reflected on his accomplishment. "Certainly I'm proud of it and feel it means something," Sawchuk said. "After all, for a shutout you're not allowed one mistake."

Although Gordie Howe's recent milestone had received more publicity, Sawchuk felt that his was the greater accomplishment. "It's much harder to get. The big scorers can make a dozen mistakes and still get a goal towards a record. A goaler makes a single goof and he has to wait until the next game to start all over. You gotta play 60 minutes to get my record."

Regarded by many as the greatest goalie ever to play the game, Sawchuk had won the Calder Trophy as the top rookie in 1950–51, and had captured the Vezina Trophy three times.

Gordie Howe was asked if he'd ever seen his teammate play a better game. "He plays them all great," answered No. 9. "He's too great a player to let anything like pressure bother him."

Sawchuk was told that he'd handled 36 shots in the game. "That many? I didn't think there were that many."

By now the 34-year-old shutout leader was relaxed and having fun. "Hey, do you know I stopped one of those shots with the butt end of my stick?" Sawchuk said, pulling off his jersey. "No kidding."

Sawchuk's record-breaking 95th shutout came in his 798th NHL game. He credited his success to his unorthodox, gorilla-like crouch in the net. "When I'm crouching low, I can keep better track of the puck through the players' legs on the screen shots," he said.

"You gotta play 60 minutes to get my record."

- Terry Sawchuk

Bobby Baun's true grit

Hockey heroes are supposed to be tough, to be able to shake off injuries and play through pain that would incapacitate lesser men. But when Bob Baun left the ice on a stretcher in the crucial sixth game of the 1964 finals, nobody expected him to come back that night in Detroit.

With the score tied 3–3 in the third period and the Leafs facing elimination, Baun was felled by a shot from the point that caught him just above the ankle.

"I heard something pop," he said afterward. Unable to get to his feet, Baun was carried to the infirmary.

The team doctor felt certain the leg was broken, but Baun refused to go to the hospital for X-rays. "Freeze it," he said.

With the game in overtime, Baun returned to the ice. After less than two minutes of play, he released a bouncing shot from the blue line that deflected off the stick of Detroit's Bill Gadsby and flipped over Terry Sawchuk's shoulder into the net.

"I forgot all about pain when I saw my blooper shoot up into the goal," Baun said in the dressing room.

Still he refused to have his leg examined, insisting the doctors wait until after the seventh game. "You don't think a little thing like this is going to make me miss the last chapter."

Although in agony, Baun played a regular shift back home in Toronto as the Leafs won 4–0 and celebrated another Stanley Cup championship.

Afterwards the doctors told him he'd been playing with a hairline fracture of the fibula. A hero's work done, Baun spent the next few weeks with his broken right leg in a cast.

"I forgot all about pain when I saw my blooper shoot up into the goal."

- Bobby Baun

Carried off the ice during the sixth game of the Cup finals, Baun returned to score the winning goal in overtime and keep Toronto's hopes alive.

Boston's inevitable Stanley Cup hero

May 10, 1970

Beantown fans had been waiting almost three decades for this moment. Just seconds into overtime, Bobby Orr took a pass from Derek Sanderson and flipped the puck past a sprawling Glenn Hall into the St. Louis goal. Tripped at the last moment, Orr went flying through the air, his arms already raised in celebration of the Bruins first Stanley Cup championship since 1941.

"I never thought there could be such a day," said Orr, who won the Conn Smythe Trophy as the most valuable player in the playoffs. "This is what every kid dreams of, scoring the winning goal in a Stanley Cup overtime final. Wow, I can't find words to express what I feel."

To the faithful thousands noisily celebrating at the Boston Garden, the hero's role played by Orr seemed almost pre-ordained. They'd adopted the remarkably gifted 22-year-old as their saviour even before his first game in a Bruin uniform. In just four seasons, Orr had fulfilled all his promise, as well as their dreams.

During the regular season Orr became the first defenceman in history to win a scoring title. Boston tied Chicago for first place in the East Division, and then swept past New York and the Hawks to meet the St. Louis Blues, winners of the West, in the finals.

Checked closely throughout the series, Orr managed just one goal: the Cup winner. But Boston's well-balanced attack proved too potent for the Blues, who went down in four straight. Centre Phil Esposito, who had finished second behind Orr in the scoring race, set playoff records with 13 goals and 27 points.

Derek Sanderson described how Orr had worked his magic for the winner: "Did you see the way he gambled to start that play? No other defenceman would have risked so much in an overtime game. But for Orr, with his natural talent and great anticipation, it was no gamble.

"Their man played it right, tried to dump the puck past Orr for a breakaway. Bobby trapped the puck. Fed it to me. I moved around the backboards until he floated into position and then fed it to him.

"I knew it was all over when the puck left his stick. You can't stop a laser beam."

Bobby Orr takes flight after beating St. Louis netminder Glenn Hall for the goal that brought Boston its first Stanley Cup since 1941.

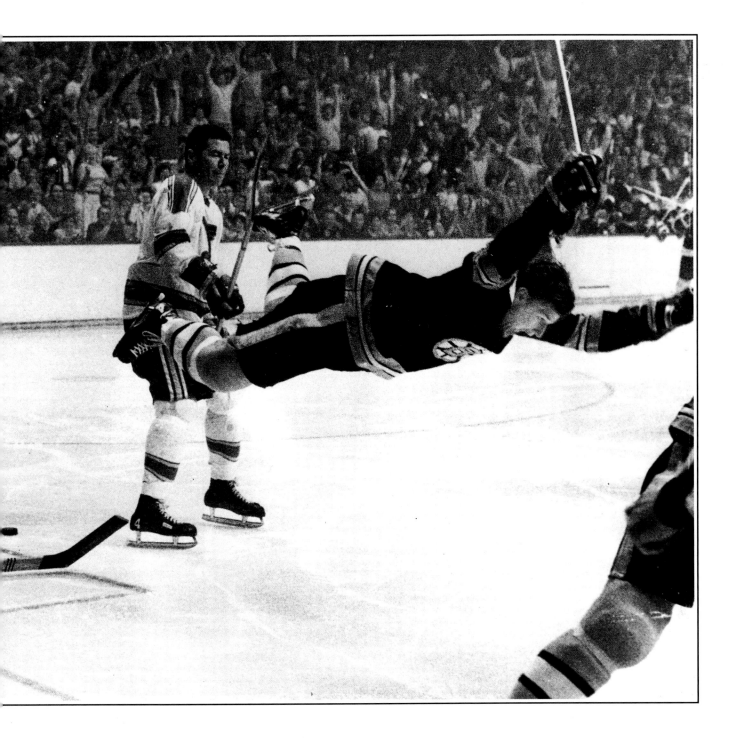

"You can't stop a laser beam."

- Derek Sanderson

Henri Richard makes amends

May 18, 1971

"The best — the best of all the ten Stanley Cups I've won," shouted Henri Richard as champagne corks popped in the Montreal dressing room. "I hope we forget everything except that we won."

Richard, the hero of the final game, was referring to the controversy he had created when he'd called Montreal coach Al MacNeil "incompetent" and "the worst coach I've ever played for." Angered by his lack of ice time, Richard's blast came after Montreal had lost the fifth game, putting the Chicago Black Hawks ahead 3–2 in the series.

Some Quebecers with separatist leanings immediately turned the remarks of the veteran star into a French-English issue. When MacNeil, who could speak no French, received death threats, he and his family were given bodyguards.

"I should have kept my mouth shut until the finals were over," Richard admitted. "Now I'm so nervous. There is so much pressure on me and the coach — we have to win."

The controversy seemed to rally the Canadiens, although it was noted that no one stepped forward to defend MacNeil. Montreal won the sixth game 4–3, and then Richard played one of the greatest games of his career to lead the Canadiens to victory in the seventh game in Chicago.

Richard tied the score at 2–2 in the second period. Then, at 2:34 of the third frame, he skated around Chicago defender Keith Magnuson and put what proved to be the winner behind goaltender Tony Esposito.

"The puck came on my skate after I got by Magnuson," Richard recounted. "I was afraid to lose control when I cut around in front of the net. I tried to fake Esposito but he pulled his stick back, so I just flipped it up."

Richard and MacNeil embraced on the ice when the final buzzer sounded. "It's just great," said MacNeil, who would soon be replaced as coach by Scotty Bowman. "He's a pro and I'm a pro. I'm glad he had the big night."

"Thanks, thanks, thanks," Richard kept shouting to his teammates. "Relieved?" he answered a reporter. "You can say that again."

Henri Richard not only scored the Cup-winning goal, but helped kill a couple of penalties as the Canadiens held off the persistent Hawks in the third period. This was the tenth of 11 championship squads he would play on, an all-time record.

*"I should have
kept my mouth
shut until the
finals were over."*

- Henri Richard

The WHA hitches a ride on the Golden Jet

June 27, 1972

With a stroke of his pen, Bobby Hull earned himself a guaranteed $2 million and provided the fledgling World Hockey Association with the instant credibility it needed to survive.

"I'm genuinely gratified," Hull told a crowd of about 5,000 delighted Winnipeggers gathered at the downtown intersection of Portage and Main. Accompanying him at the ceremonial signing of his contract was Winnipeg Jets owner Ben Hatskin (who had pursued hockey's Golden Jet over several months) as well as Hull's wife Joanne and three of the Hulls' five children — sons Bobby, Blake and Brett, who would one day earn his own millions playing hockey for the St. Louis Blues.

The deal included a lump payment of $1 million from the WHA, for which Hull would perform various publicity functions, as well as $250,000 a year from the Jets for each of the next five years. At the end of the contract, Hull would have the option of continuing to play for the same $250,000 annual salary, or earning $100,000 a year as a fulltime Jets executive.

"There's never been a sports contract like this one," said Hull's agent Harvey Weinberg, a Chicago chartered accountant. "Bob is guaranteed $2 million even if the WHA never plays a game."

Weinberg told reporters that Hull's former employers, the Chicago Black Hawks, hadn't come close to matching the offer from the WHA. In 15 seasons with the Hawks, Hull had scored 604 goals, a total surpassed only by Gordie Howe's 786, and he had twice been named the winner of the Hart Trophy as the league's most valuable player.

The contract placed Hull among the highest-paid performers in professional sport. Basketball's Wilt Chamberlain was then earning about $250,000; baseball's Hank Aaron was making $200,000.

"I look at it this way," Hull joked to his Winnipeg audience. "I've got $2 million in my pocket and don't go to work until October 1."

Jets owner Ben Hatskin said that even at the price paid, the deal "was a hell of a bargain." Bobby Hull's signing had just given the WHA a fighting chance.

> **"There's never been a sports contract like this one."**

Seen here with the Hull family, Jets owner Ben Hatskin predicted: "Bobby Hull will sell hockey in every one of our franchise cities."

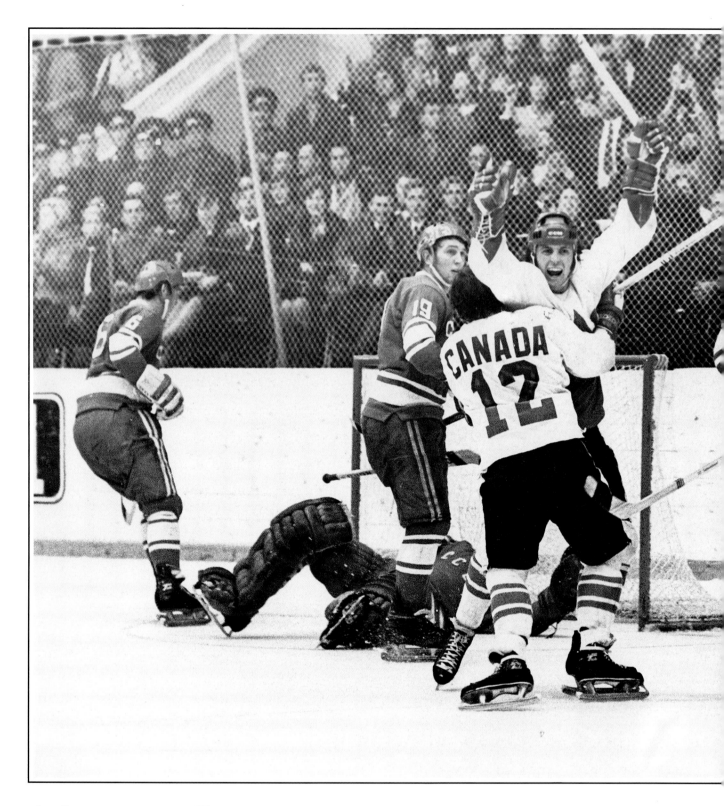

*At that moment millions
of Canadians danced
and hugged and kissed
in celebration.*

"Henderson scores for Canada!"

September 28, 1972

A jubilant Paul Henderson is hugged by teammate Yvan Cournoyer after scoring the most famous goal in hockey history. Henderson beat Soviet goaltender Vladislav Tretiak with just 34 seconds remaining on the clock.

Canadians who are old enough to remember will never forget *the Goal*.

"Here's a shot. Henderson makes a wild stab for it and falls," broadcaster Foster Hewitt breathlessly described the action at Moscow's Palace of Sport. "Here's another shot. Right in front. They score! Henderson scores for Canada!"

At that moment millions of exultant Canadians danced and hugged and kissed in a scene that reminded many of the celebration at the end of World War II. Never before or since in the life of the country has a single sporting moment meant so much to so many.

Paul Henderson's goal sealed a remarkable comeback victory for Team Canada over a Soviet squad that had pushed Canada to the brink of defeat in the eight-game summit series. After winning two and tying another of the four games played on Canadian soil, the Soviet Nationals had seemingly assured themselves of victory by winning game five in Moscow.

None of this was supposed to happen. Team Canada, composed of the NHL's greatest stars, had been expected to romp to victory. The success of the Soviets stunned Canadians, who had always unquestioningly believed in their country's hockey supremacy.

Team Canada restored their faith by fighting back to win the final three games, all on late goals by Paul Henderson, a talented but not usually spectacular 29-year-old left winger whom fate had singled out for the hero's role. In the third period of the final game, Team Canada came from three goals back to tie the score at 5–5. Then, with 34 seconds remaining on the clock, Henderson beat Soviet netminder Vladislav Tretiak for *the Goal*.

"I found myself with the puck in front of the net," remembered Henderson of the moment that placed him among the pantheon of Canadian heroes. "Tretiak made one stop and the puck came right back to me. There was some room under him, so I poked the puck through.

"When I saw it go in, I just went bonkers." Back home, millions of thrilled, proud and tremendously relieved Canadians joined in.

Because of his diabetes,
he had always been
forced to out-perform
everyone else.

Clarke breaks 100 and wins a Hart

March 29, 1973

In four seasons in the NHL, Clarke had averaged almost a point a game with 294 points, 114 of them goals. At first he was reluctant to discuss his diabetes with reporters. "If I didn't play well, I didn't want them saying it was because of that," Clarke said.

Although regarded as an exceptionally promising young player, Bobby Clarke of the Philadelphia Flyers went from being a relative unknown to one of the game's biggest stars during the 1972–73 season.

A diabetic who had to take daily insulin shots, Clarke attracted attention even before the start of the regular season when he played a prominent role in Team Canada's famous summit series with the Soviets. Clarke charged fearlessly into corners to set up scoring opportunities for linemates Paul Henderson and Ron Ellis. Many felt that he tipped the balance in favour of Team Canada when he delivered a vicious slash that broke the ankle of Soviet star Valeri Kharlamov.

Clarke made no apologies for such hard-nosed tactics. Because of his diabetes, he had always been the underdog, forced to out-perform and out-hustle everyone else to prove that his illness wasn't holding him back.

On March 29, the truculent, blond-haired centreman scored two goals against Atlanta to become the first player on an expansion team to record 100 points in a season. The campaign also saw him score his 100th NHL career goal and become, at age 23, the league's youngest team captain.

Clarke finished the season with 37 goals and 67 assists for second place in the scoring race behind Phil Esposito. But he left the Boston veteran far behind in the voting for the Hart Memorial Trophy, awarded to the player judged most valuable to his team. Clarke received 158 votes compared to 96 for Esposito, who was runner-up.

Winning the Hart was another first for a player with an expansion team. Clarke was asked if this meant he was the world's best hockey player.

"Are you kidding?" the modest young star replied. "If it went to the best, Bobby Orr would win it every year, hands down."

"What a year!" exults Canada Cup hero

September 15, 1976

Darryl Sittler had just put the perfect finish to an admittedly unexplainable, totally improbable and altogether wonderful year. In February, the Toronto captain had scored a record ten points in a match against Boston. Then, in the playoffs, he'd potted five goals in a game against the Philadelphia Flyers. And now, best of all, Sittler had scored the winning goal in the Canada Cup.

"What a year!" the champagne-soaked hero exulted after Canada's 5–4 overtime victory over the Czechoslovakian national team. "How do you explain one guy having a year like I've had? The big nights just came my way for some reason which I'll never be able to explain. They've all been incredible, all big thrills, but there was something pretty special about this one, scoring a goal that won a world championship for a team representing your country. Not much could top that, could it?"

Stocked with Canada's greatest players — including Bobby Orr, Bobby Hull, Guy Lafleur and Marcel Dionne — Team Canada lost only one of its seven games in the six-team tournament. Thanks to Sittler's marker at 11:33 of overtime, the best-of-three final against the Czechs (the reigning world amateur champions) was won in two straight games.

Sittler told how a tip from Don Cherry, one of Canada's four co-coaches, gave him an advantage when he broke in on Czech netminder Vladimir Dzurilla for the decisive score. "Cherry said the Czech goalie was cutting down the angles so much our shots were all hitting him," the 26-year-old centre recounted. "Don suggested we try delaying a bit, taking an extra stride or two and then shooting."

Working on a line with Marcel Dionne and fellow Leaf Lanny McDonald, Sittler fielded a pass from Dionne and moved down the left wing into the Czech zone. Just as Cherry had predicted, Dzurilla came out to cut down the angle. "I held it until I was in pretty deep, and there was a hole on the far side. I shot for it and in it went.

"I've had some big nights in the NHL, broke some records, but nothing could compare with this," Sittler said. "To score a goal like this, well, it's just unbelievable."

Sittler told how a tip from Don Cherry gave him an advantage.

Darryl Sittler raises his stick in celebration after beating Czech goalie Vladimir Dzurilla for the overtime goal that won the tournament. Team Canada was stocked with Canada's greatest players, including Guy Lafleur and Bobby Hull (above).

The Miracle on Main Street

February 22, 1980

Commentators instantly dubbed it the Miracle on Main Street, the biggest upset in Olympic hockey history.

Somehow a collection of unknown American collegians managed a 4–3 comeback defeat of a Soviet squad that included several of the world's greatest players, superstars named Maltsev, Krutov and Tretiak, who had often defeated the best the NHL could send against them.

The Americans did it with the same combination of relentless backchecking and spectacular goaltending by Jim Craig that had earned them an unbeaten record to that point late in the tournament. As they faced off against the Soviets at a packed Olympic Field House on Lake Placid's Main Street, millions of their compatriots, many of them new converts to the game, tuned in anxiously at home.

Twice the Americans had to fight back from one-goal deficits. Behind 3–2 at the end of the second period, they tied it in the third on a power play goal by Mark Johnson. A minute and 21 seconds later captain Mark Eruzione put them ahead when he slapped a high slapshot past Soviet goaltender Vladimir Myshkin, who had replaced an unusually shaky Vladislav Tretiak earlier in the game. With Craig kicking out shot after shot in the dying minutes, the Americans held on to win.

The post-game celebration in the dressing room was interrupted by a call from U.S. president Jimmy Carter. "He told us we made our country proud," repeated coach Herb Brooks. "He said we had lived up to the ideals of this country."

They had also inspired a wave of enthusiasm for hockey in the United States that is still being felt. Within a year, ten of the Olympians joined NHL teams, swelling the ranks of Americans in the league. Among them were Jim Craig, Mark Johnson, Steve Christoff and Neal Broten, who went on to become the first U.S.-born player to score more than 100 points in an NHL season.

Two days after defeating the Soviets, the Americans captured the gold medal with a 4–2 victory over Finland. The miracle was complete.

> ## "He told us we made our country proud."
>
> ### - U.S. coach Herb Brooks quoting Jimmy Carter

The Americans celebrate their stunning upset victory over a Soviet squad that had won every Olympic gold medal in the past 20 years.

Two victors, one Conn Smythe Trophy

May 16, 1982

Posed with the Conn Smythe Trophy on his knee, a beaming Mike Bossy was happy to admit that his teammate Bryan Trottier was equally deserving of the honour. "But I won't lie," he laughed. "I'm honest in saying that I'm very pleased that I won."

Trottier, who had won the award given to the most valuable player in the playoffs two years before, pretended to be hurt at the injustice of being passed over. "Aw, he's just lucky," said Bossy's centreman and best friend.

Bossy and Trottier. The duo dominated the playoffs as the New York Islanders rolled to their third consecutive Stanley Cup. Vancouver coach Roger Neilson, whose Canucks fell in four straight games to the Islanders in the final, called Trottier the best player in the world, and named Bossy the game's greatest goal scorer.

Bossy scored 17 goals in the playoffs, and put seven in the net in the final to tie a record held by Jean Beliveau. Trottier contributed 23 playoff assists, breaking Bobby Orr's old mark by three.

Bossy's overtime winner in the opener (he'd also scored the tying goal) permanently shifted the momentum to the Islanders. "If we could have won that first game, I think we could have turned the series around," lamented Canuck Tiger Williams.

In the final match, played in Vancouver, Bossy scored the Cup winner on a power play in the second period. The score was tied 1–1 when he beat Canuck goaltender Richard Brodeur on a setup by Trottier. He added another power play goal (his sixth of the finals) exactly three minutes later to complete the Islander scoring. Trottier assisted on that one, too.

The kibitzing continued at the post-game press conference. Bossy was asked what he would do with the car that went along with the Conn Smythe Trophy. "I'm still hoping to fix the flat on the first one I won," he quipped in reference to his prize for being named the outstanding player of the league all-star game.

"He's lucky," repeated a laughing Trottier. "No, really, I'm proud of him. I just hope that in the next playoff, I'm the one who gets the passes."

Mike Bossy celebrates after beating Vancouver netminder Richard Brodeur for the Cup-winning goal in the fourth game of the finals. Awarded the Conn Smythe Trophy as playoff MVP, Bossy scored 17 goals in post-season play.

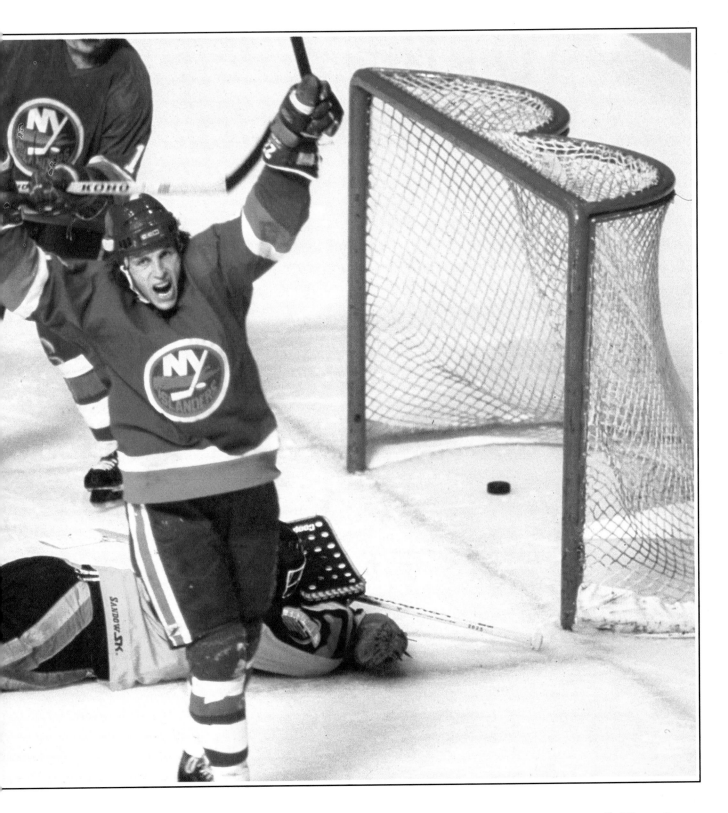

Bossy and Trottier dominated the playoffs as the Islanders rolled to the Cup.

Oilers win with the buddy system

May 19, 1984

Friendship, Mark Messier felt certain, was the biggest reason the Edmonton Oilers were able to dethrone the New York Islanders and capture their first Stanley Cup.

"I know it sounds corny, but that was a big inspiration to the team," said Messier, who was awarded the Conn Smythe Trophy as the most valuable playoff performer. "If we'd lost to the Islanders again, several of us wouldn't be here next season. Well, we all want to stay together."

Messier and his best friend Wayne Gretzky led the Oilers to a convincing five-game triumph that dashed the Islanders dream of equalling Montreal's five consecutive championships from 1956 to 1960. Gretzky topped all playoff scorers with 13 goals and 22 assists, while Messier contributed 26 points and scored a sensational goal in the third game of the final that helped turn the tide against the Islanders.

After having split the first two games, the Oilers were trailing 2–1 in the third match when Messier turned on his tremendous speed and went the length of the ice before powering a shot past Islanders goalie Billy Smith. The Oilers never looked back, racking up a 7–2 score by the final buzzer. Edmonton won by another 7–2 decision two nights later, and then claimed the Cup with a 5–2 triumph in front of 17,500 delirious fans at Northlands Coliseum.

Edmonton's victory avenged the humiliating four-game sweep handed them by the Islanders in the final the year before. In response to that defeat, coach Glen Sather had insisted that his high-scoring troops concentrate more on defence.

The Oilers ground out a 1–0 decision in the opening game of the final. "No one will ever know how much that did for the confidence of this team," said Sather. "It showed our guys that we could play what was supposed to be the Islanders game, tight defensive hockey."

Wayne Gretzky agreed with Messier that the closeness of the Edmonton players had made a large contribution to the victory, and was certain to pay future dividends. "We've matured together," said the 23-year-old captain. "Most of us are pretty young guys. Now that we've made the breakthrough, the best is yet to come."

> "If we'd lost to the Islanders, several of us wouldn't be here next season."
>
> - Mark Messier

Despite the presence of Wayne Gretzky in Edmonton's formidable lineup, Mark Messier was thought by many to be the heart and soul of the team. Here he shows off the Conn Smythe Trophy, which he won as playoff MVP.

Doug Jarvis becomes the new Iron Man

December 26, 1986

> *"I can't believe the guy went that long without catching a cold."*
>
> *- Gordie Howe*

"It's an individual-type thing, a sidelight," said Doug Jarvis of the Hartford Whalers after playing in his record 915th consecutive game, eclipsing the old Iron Man mark held by Garry Unger. "You just have to go to the rink and put it out of your mind."

Although Jarvis may not have wanted to dwell on his accomplishment, it was viewed with awe by others. "It's an unbelievable record," commented Gordie Howe. "I can't believe the guy went that long without catching a cold."

Whalers coach Jack Evans said the new record would "be very difficult to break, because of the number of games and the travel" faced by current players.

Jarvis, a 31-year-old centre renowned for his penalty-killing ability, hadn't missed a game since entering the NHL with Montreal in 1975. He had celebrated four Stanley Cup championships with the Canadiens before being traded to Washington in September 1982. In 1984, Jarvis captured the Frank Selke Trophy, presented to the best defensive forward in the NHL. He was acquired by Hartford in December 1985.

Just 5'9" and 170 pounds, Jarvis took a tremendous pounding throughout his career, which made his achievement all the more remarkable. "Doug Jarvis exemplifies the type of person who puts the team ahead of the individual," said Bryan Murray, his coach in Washington. "He will sacrifice the body and take a check every time to be sure the puck gets out of the zone."

At the conclusion of his record-breaking season, Jarvis was named the winner of the Bill Masterton Memorial Trophy, presented annually to the NHL player thought to best demonstrate "the qualities of perseverance, sportsmanship and dedication to hockey."

Three games into the next season, Jarvis finally sat one out — not because he was injured or sick, but because by now the thirteen-year veteran was visibly slowing down, the end of his career drawing near. On October 11, 1987, he was told not to dress for that night's game against Boston. The consecutive-game record that many believe will never be broken had ended at 964 games.

Jarvis broke the Iron Man record of 914 games held by Garry Unger, whose streak began in the 1967-68 season and ended during the 1979-80 campaign.

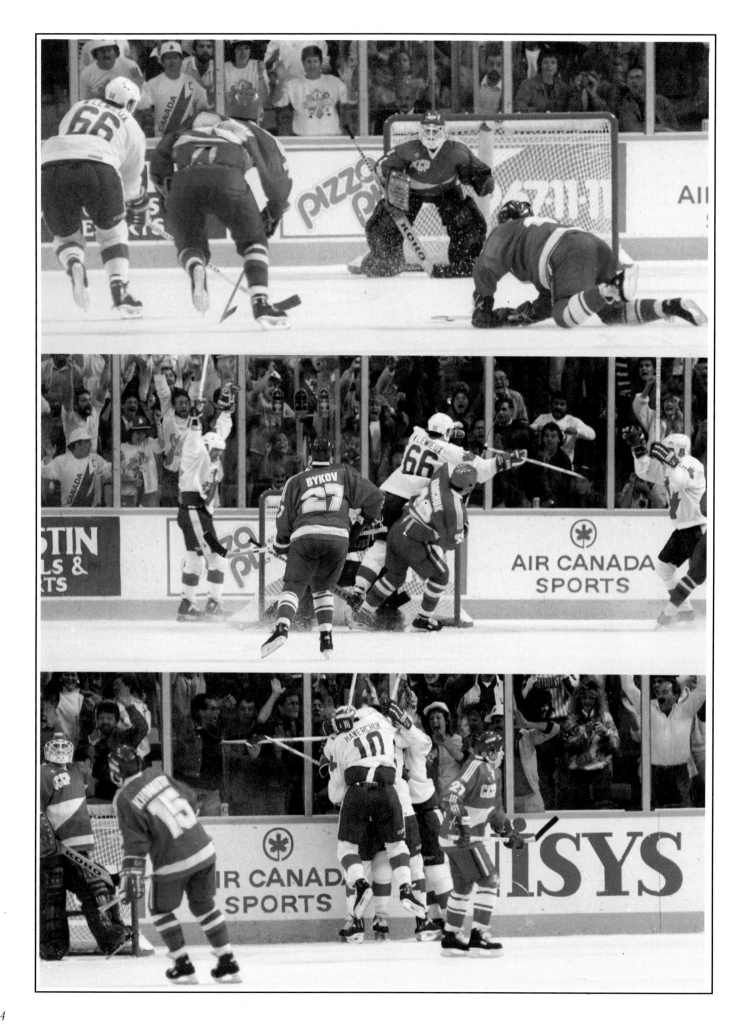

Lemieux and Gretzky spark Canada Cup win

September 15, 1987

The two greatest players in the world again combined their remarkable talents.

None of the games could possibly have been closer — or more exciting. One writer described the championship-round confrontation between Canada and the Soviets in the fourth Canada Cup as "probably the most thrilling, brilliant, continuous display of hockey ever seen."

The Soviets won the first match of the best-of-three series five minutes into overtime. Team Canada took the next one after 30 minutes of extra play when Mario Lemieux redirected a Wayne Gretzky shot into the net. In the deciding game, played at Hamilton's Copps Coliseum, the two greatest players in the world again combined their remarkable talents to determine the tournament's outcome.

With the score tied 5–5 and less than two minutes remaining in the third period, Lemieux poked the puck away from Soviet defenceman Igor Kravchuk along the boards in the Canadian end.

Gretzky rushed in and took possession, then started up ice with defenceman Larry Murphy keeping pace to his right and Lemieux trailing a step behind.

"I thought he was going to pass the puck to Murphy," recounted Lemieux. "The other defenceman went for Wayne and that left me free."

Gretzky put a dazzling fake on a Soviet defender and then slid a pass back to the 21-year-old Pittsburgh Penguins superstar. "As I skated in I saw that the top shelf was open," Lemieux said. "I was just trying to find a hole."

Lemieux took aim and snapped a rising wrist shot into the top right corner over the shoulder of Soviet goalie Sergei Mylnikov. It was his eleventh goal of the series, nine of them scored on assists by Gretzky.

Like the previous two matches in the final, this one ended in a 6–5 score. The Canadians were forced to regroup after the Russians jumped out to a 3–0 lead in the first eight minutes of play. Before Lemieux's winning goal, both clubs had scored 16 times.

Gretzky, the captain, offered a brief explanation for the Canadians comeback win. "Guts, pride and desire," he said. "We refused to be licked."

After a beautiful set-up by Gretzky, Mario Lemieux breaks in for the winning goal.

Lafleur's triumphant homecoming

February 4, 1989

"It was destiny for me to quit, and I guess it was destiny for me to come back," said Guy Lafleur before his eagerly awaited return to the Montreal Forum as a member of the New York Rangers.

The leading scorer in the glorious history of the Canadiens, Lafleur had played on five Stanley Cup winners in 14 seasons with the *bleu, blanc et rouge* before retiring in November 1984. Now, at the age of 37 and having already been voted into the Hockey Hall of Fame, he was in the midst of a successful comeback with the Rangers. On New York's previous visit to Montreal in December, Lafleur had been injured and unable to play. This would be his first return to the Forum as a player in more than four years.

Ticket scalpers were asking $400 for a pair of choice seats for the home-coming of the star known as the Flower. When Lafleur stepped on the ice before the start of the game, he received a two-minute standing ovation. Chants of "Guy! Guy! Guy!..." drowned out the national anthems.

Each time he jumped the boards, the chant would begin again. Although the fans wanted Montreal to win, they also hoped Lafleur would show them the blazing speed and powerful shot they remembered so well.

To their delight, Lafleur assisted on a Ranger goal in the first period. Then, in the second frame, the years magically fell away and the Lafleur of their memory returned.

Left alone in front of the Montreal net, he picked up a rebound and whipped a shot past a prone Patrick Roy. "Guy! Guy! Guy!..." roared the ecstatic crowd.

About six minutes later, Lafleur took a pass at centre ice, sped around a defenceman and blasted a shot between Roy's legs. The fans stomped and cheered and chanted their adoration as Lafleur was mobbed by his teammates.

Chosen the game's second star after a 7–5 Montreal victory, Lafleur skated onto the ice and waved his appreciation as the fans picked up the familiar chorus once again. After more than four years, Flower power was back and in full bloom at the Forum.

Ticket scalpers were asking $400 for a pair of choice seats for the return of the Flower.

Lafleur brought the crowd to its feet when he picked up a rebound and beat Canadiens netminder Patrick Roy (at right) for his first goal at the Forum in more than four years. Above, the Flower attempts to get by Montreal defenceman Jyrki Lumme.

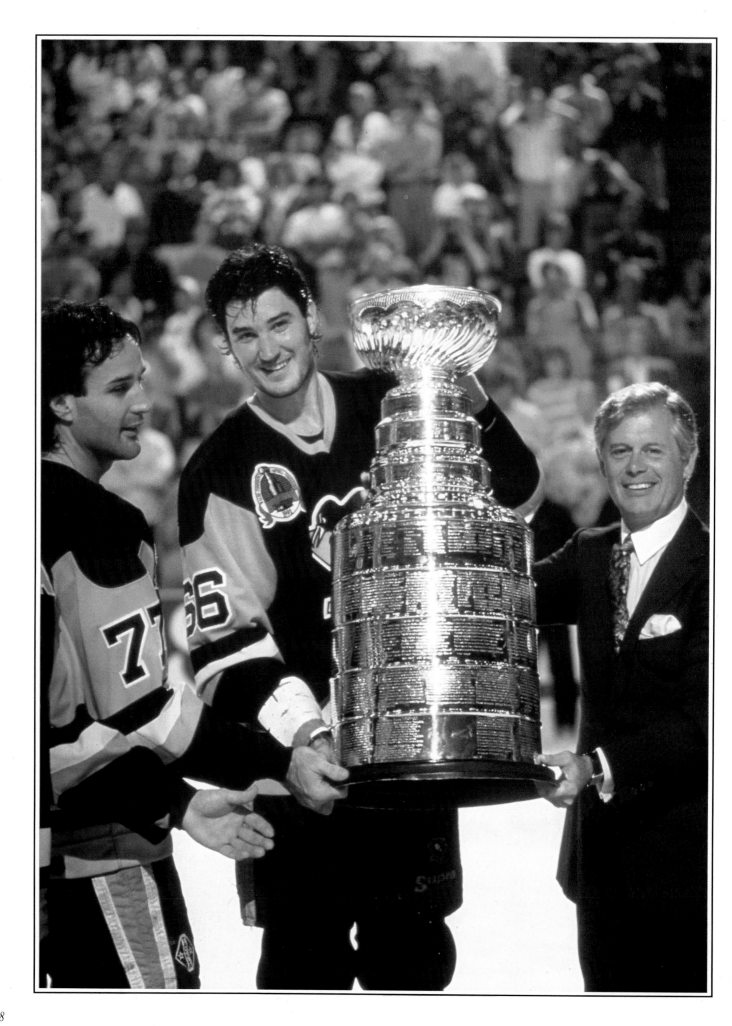

Lemieux carries Pens on his bad back

May 25, 1991

> **"This feeling is greater than I ever thought. It's got to be the ultimate dream."**
>
> *- Mario Lemieux*

After undergoing back surgery and missing more than half of the regular season, Mario Lemieux returned to lead the Penguins to their first Stanley Cup championship. His brilliance in the playoffs earned him the Conn Smythe Trophy.

Considering that Mario Lemieux was bedridden at the start of the season, unable even to walk after surgery to repair a herniated disk, his performance in the playoffs was nothing short of miraculous. After missing 50 games of the regular season, Lemieux routinely outscored and outplayed everyone else on the ice in leading the Pittsburgh Penguins to the first Stanley Cup championship in the team's 24-year history.

"This feeling is greater than I ever thought," said Lemieux, who was awarded the Conn Smythe Trophy as the most valuable player in the post-season. "It means everything — to be part of a championship team. It's got to be the ultimate dream."

Dubbed "Super Mario" by headline writers, Lemieux led all playoff scorers with 16 goals and 28 assists for 44 points, second only to the 47 points compiled by Wayne Gretzky with the Edmonton Oilers in 1985. In the six-game final with the Minnesota North Stars, Lemieux scored five goals and added seven assists, and was named the first star in three matches. His aching back forced him to sit out the third game, which Pittsburgh lost.

"My job is to go on the ice and score a big goal at the right time, make the play and lead the team to victory," said Lemieux.

He did exactly that in the second game against Minnesota, scoring a magnificent goal that spurred the Penguins to a crucial victory after they had dropped the opener. In the Cup-clincher at Bloomington, Lemieux scored in the first period and added three assists to lead the Pens to an 8–0 trashing of the North Stars.

There were those who believed that Lemieux had now proved himself to be the dominant player in the game, greater even than archrival Wayne Gretzky.

"We were saying before the series that Mario was a great hockey player, but until you win a championship, there are always going to be doubts," said his teammate Paul Coffey. "It's unfair but that's the way it is.

"There are no doubts any more. The great ones find a way to do it. And he did."

Like father, like son: Hull captures the Hart

June 5, 1991

> *"When I was a kid watching my dad play, I always dreamed of being in that category."*
>
> *- Brett Hull*

"This brings me a little closer to what he has done," said Brett Hull, nodding in the direction of his beaming father at the annual NHL awards dinner in Toronto. "It's a real feather in my cap."

It was 25 years since Bobby Hull, the legendary Golden Jet, had stood before a similar gathering and accepted his second straight Hart Trophy as the National Hockey League's most valuable player. Now the Hulls had become the first father-son MVP winners, possibly in any pro sport.

Brett Hull, dubbed the Golden Brett, had just completed a campaign in which he scored a league-leading 86 goals. His first 50 goals came in just 49 games, making him only the fifth player to score 50 in the first 50 or fewer matches. It was an accomplishment even his father hadn't managed.

In the past three seasons, the younger Hull had scored 199 goals. His total of 72 the season before also led the league. At the age of 26, Brett Hull ranked among the elite players in the game.

"When I was a kid watching my dad play, I always dreamed of being in that category," he told an interviewer.

Although equally gifted as a goal scorer, Brett Hull became a much different type of player than his father — more of an opportunist. The elder Hull most often scored on rink-long rushes or after unleashing his fearsome slapshot from far out. But his son preferred to dart into openings, looking for passes from teammates.

"He's incredible, the way he fades in and out of the play," said Red Wings assistant coach Doug MacLean. "He'll just slide in, get away a shot and he's gone."

Reporters wondered if by winning the Hart, Brett Hull felt that he had emerged from the long shadow cast by his father.

"Maybe one day I will be equal to my dad, but never better," the Golden Brett answered. "I will always be Bobby's son."

Bobby and Brett Hull at the NHL awards dinner in Toronto. The senior Hull won the Hart Trophy as league MVP in 1964-65 and 1965-66.

802 and counting for Gretzky

March 23, 1994

It's not every hockey star who gets serenaded by a famous Hollywood actress after a milestone goal. But then there is only one Wayne Gretzky.

While Goldie Hawn finished a chorus of "Oh, What a Night" outside the Los Angeles Kings dressing room, Gretzky was inside telling reporters how it felt to have passed Gordie Howe to become the NHL's all-time goal-scoring leader.

"The best," Gretzky said of his 61st NHL record. "There is no comparison. The ones that are the best are the hardest to break. Somebody is going to have to play 16 years at 50 goals a year to do it."

Gretzky's historic 802nd career goal came at 14:47 of the second period on a power play, when he redirected a pass from teammate Marty McSorley past Vancouver Canucks goaltender Kirk McLean. Gretzky leaped for joy and then danced across the ice of the Los Angeles Forum as 16,005 fans paid a long, noisy tribute.

Play was stopped as Gretzky was joined on the ice by his parents and wife Janet, team owner Bruce McNall and Gary Bettman, the NHL commissioner. The ten-minute ceremony included a video retrospective of Gretzky's career.

"You always were the Great One," Bettman said after presenting Gretzky with a book containing the scoresheets from every game in which he scored a goal. "Tonight, you became the greatest."

Hockey's career goal-scoring leader displayed his usual modesty when handed the microphone. "As I have said many times, it's the greatest game in the world. I would like to thank my mother and my father and my dear, beloved Janet. Thank you all."

Watching on television at his home in Michigan, Gordie Howe offered his congratulations and suggested that his 33-year-old successor keep going until he got to at least 1,000 goals. Howe had set the old record in 1,767 regular-season games; Gretzky beat him in 650 fewer matches.

"I see 900, I see a thousand," said the newly crowned Greatest One as Goldie Hawn completed her musical tribute. "I don't know if I'll get there, but I'll give it an effort. My life is hockey."

Wayne Gretzky addresses the crowd during a break in play after shattering Gordie Howe's all-time goal-scoring record. But the night was not a complete success for No. 99. His Kings lost 6–3 to Vancouver.

"I see 900, I see a thousand."

- *Wayne Gretzky*

"I often look at those guys who can whistle and laugh before a game and shake my head. Me? I'm plain miserable before every game."

- Chicago goalie Glenn Hall

Big goals, great saves, streaks and longshots

Dawson City and the call of the Stanley Cup

Boyle and his men set out by dog sled on the first leg of their long trek.

It's a story straight out of a Jack London novel, complete with dog teams and raging blizzards, a flamboyant hero known as the King of the Klondike and a hardy group of hockey-playing gold miners who undertook a perilous 4,400-mile journey to challenge for the Stanley Cup.

Hockey's most incredible saga began when Joe Boyle, an adventurer from Woodstock, Ontario, headed north in the Klondike Stampede of '98 and quickly earned his fortune as well as the royal moniker. An ice hockey enthusiast, Boyle organized the Dawson City Nuggets and then issued a challenge to the mighty Ottawa Silver Seven, reigning Stanley Cup champions and the greatest team of the era.

Boyle and his men set out by dog sled for the port of Skagway on the first leg of their long trek to Ottawa. It was said that temperatures dipped to 20 degrees below zero Fahrenheit, and that some of the men developed blisters on their feet and had to continue on in their stocking feet.

They missed their boat connection at Skagway by two hours, and sat idly for five days before embarking for Seattle. Then it was on to Vancouver, where they caught an eastbound train. "All along the route the Klondikers received expressions of good will from hockey enthusiasts who apparently are a unit in their desire to see the Yukon gentlemen beat Ottawa," reported the Ottawa *Journal*.

Amid much fanfare, the team arrived in Ottawa January 12. Boyle requested that the series be postponed a week to give his men time to recover from their journey and get in some practice. But the Silver Seven refused, insisting that the first game of the best-of-three series take place the next day as scheduled.

Even had they been rested, it was soon obvious that the Nuggets would have been no match for the Silver Seven, who won the opener 9–2. Three days later, "One-Eyed" Frank McGee, the game's most famous star, scored 14 goals as Ottawa humiliated Dawson City 23–2.

No team in Stanley Cup history has ever taken a worse beating. But it can also be said that no other challenger has ever had such a novel adventure.

The lure of gold had sent the members of the Dawson City Nuggets north to the Yukon; the challenge of competing for Lord Stanley's silver bowl brought them south again on hockey's greatest adventure.

Joe Malone notches his still-standing seven

January 31, 1920

An elderly "Phantom" Joe Malone was once asked to compare the era when he was setting scoring records with the modern game. "I used to play practically the whole game," he recalled. "We'd have two or three utilitymen on the bench, but they'd only get on if somebody was hurt. So I think I had a lot more chances to score."

Over the years the long list of records once held by Malone has been whittled down until only one remains. Syd Howe, Red Berenson and Darryl Sittler have all come within a goal, but no one has ever equalled Malone's achievement of scoring seven times in a single NHL match.

A fast, effortless skater famed for his ability to stickhandle through an entire team, Malone scored his seven for the Quebec Bulldogs in a game against the Toronto St. Pats. He put three in the net in a span of 120 seconds.

The Phantom notched 146 goals in 125 regular-season games over the course of his seven-year NHL career. In the league's inaugural season, 1917–18, he beat goaltenders 44 times in 20 games (he missed two matches) while playing for the Montreal Canadiens, a single-season record that stood until 1945, when Rocket Richard scored 50 goals in 50 games.

The Toronto goalie Malone victimized was Jakey Forbes, whom he regarded as one of the best in the business, along with Clint Benedict and Georges Vezina.

"The goalies used to stand up more in those days," he said. "I remember pulling the goalie out a lot. Now they have such scrambles around the goal that most times you have to wait for the red light to go on before you know there's been a goal scored."

One perhaps fanciful account of Malone's outing against the St. Pats had it that the desperate Toronto squad finally employed two goaltenders in an attempt to stop him. The game, which Quebec won 10–6, was played outdoors in temperatures that dipped to –25 degrees Fahrenheit.

Malone, whose top salary was $2,000, expressed little nostalgia for the old days. "Today's game is faster, and the players are better than we were," insisted the only man ever to score seven goals in an NHL game.

> **"I used to play practically the whole game."**
>
> *- "Phantom" Joe Malone*

Joe Malone is seated front and centre (behind the canine mascot) in the team photo of the Quebec Bulldogs, Stanley Cup champions in 1912–13. Malone played seven seasons in the old National Hockey Association before the league evolved into the NHL in 1917. He scored a record 44 goals in 20 games while with the Montreal Canadiens in 1917–18. After returning to the Bulldogs for the 1919–20 campaign, Malone notched his seven goals against Toronto.

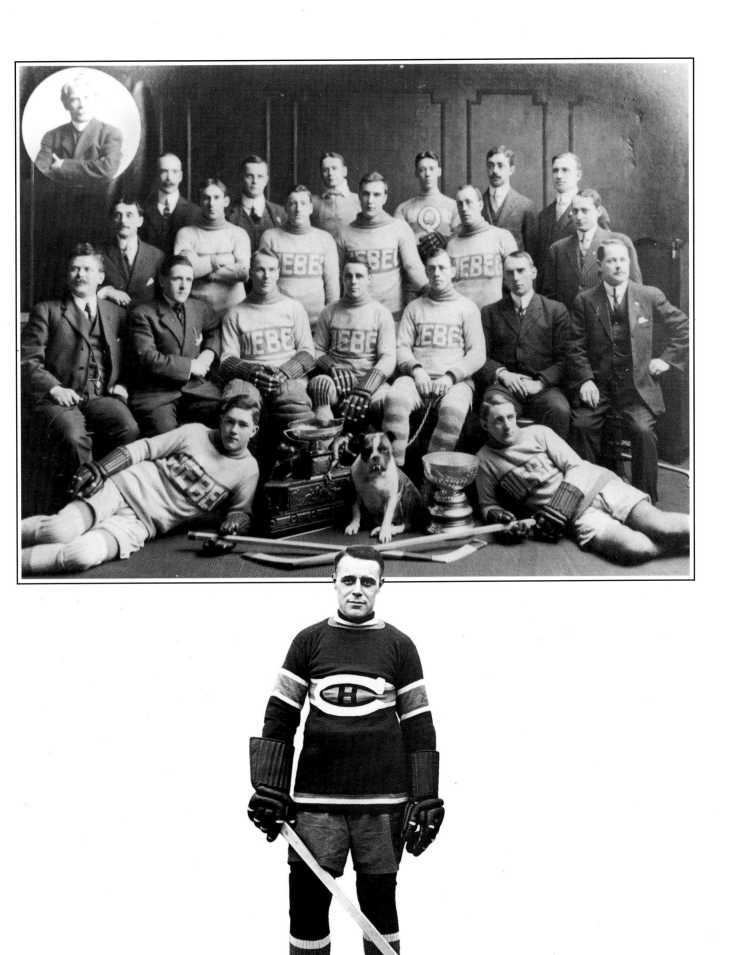

Mud Bruneteau ends the longest game

March 24–25, 1936

Before the start of their first-round playoff series, the Montreal Maroons and the Detroit Red Wings were judged to be fairly evenly matched. Montreal, the defending Stanley Cup champions, had finished in first place in the Canadian Division, while Detroit concluded the schedule atop the American Division.

Hockey was a much tighter, defence-oriented game in those days. So no one was too surprised when there was no scoring in the first and second periods of the opener in Montreal. But when the scoreless tie continued through the third period and on into overtime, the restless patrons began checking their watches.

Both goaltenders, Lorne Chabot for the Maroons and Norm Smith for the Wings, were tested time and again. Smith made a miraculous stop close in on the dangerous Hooley Smith. Chabot kicked back a blistering drive from flashy Wing centreman Martin Barry.

The players battled on to the point of collapse through a second, third, fourth, fifth and into a sixth overtime period. After 4:46 of the sixth extra session, Montreal and Detroit owned the record for the longest playoff game, breaking the old mark of 164 minutes, 46 seconds, set on April 3, 1933, when Toronto defeated Boston 1–0.

"They fed us sugar dipped in brandy to keep us going," remembered Norm Smith, who was called upon to make 90 saves.

Finally, mercifully, the struggle ended at 16:30 of the sixth overtime after 176 minutes, 30 seconds, of play. The time was 2:25 a.m., just over five hours and 51 minutes after the game began.

Modere "Mud" Bruneteau, a 21-year-old rookie whose legs were perhaps stronger than those of the Montreal defenders, took a pass from teammate Hec Kilrea, deked around Chabot, who had made 66 saves, and deposited the puck into the open net.

"Everybody was so stunned there was a ten-second pause and then they all broke loose," Smith said of his teammates' reaction to Bruneteau's winner.

Montreal was unable to recover from the ordeal and lost the best-of-five series in consecutive games. Excused from practice the day after history's longest game, the refreshed Red Wings marched on to their first Stanley Cup championship.

The players battled on through a second, third, fourth, fifth and into a sixth overtime period.

The winning goal by Modere "Mud" Bruneteau (pictured at right) was the rookie's first in playoff action. Detroit went on to beat Toronto in the finals and capture their first of two consecutive Stanley Cups.

61

*All bets were on
Toronto to make
short work of the
Black Hawks.*

From chumps to champs

Chicago coach Bill Stewart, the first American to coach a Cup-winning team, was carried to the dressing room by his players after the final game. The Hawks had a record eight U.S.-born players on the championship roster.

It wasn't even supposed to be close. All bets were on the powerful Toronto Maple Leafs, who had topped the Canadian Division and led the league in scoring, to make short work of the Chicago Black Hawks in the 1938 Stanley Cup final.

How the Hawks had gotten as far as they did was a mystery. They'd won only 14 games during the regular season, finishing well below the .500 mark in third spot in the American Division. Then, somehow, they'd squeaked past the Montreal Canadiens and the New York Americans in the preliminary rounds of the playoffs.

But the Hawks string of miracles looked to be at an end as the teams skated onto the ice in Toronto for a controversial start to the best-of-five series. Tempers had flared before the game when Toronto boss Conn Smythe refused Chicago's request to replace their regular goaltender, Mike Karakas, unable to play because of a broken toe, with New York Ranger goalie Davey Kerr, who was in attendance and offered to fill in. Instead, Smythe insisted they use pint-sized Alfie Moore, a poorly regarded minor leaguer owned by the New York Americans.

Moore surprised everyone with his magnificent play as the Hawks won 3–1. At game's end, he thumbed his nose at the Leaf bench.

The Leafs rebounded to take the second game 5–1. Then Karakas, who was largely responsible for getting the Hawks into the finals, returned for game three and turned the tide as Chicago won 2–1. Two nights later, with the Cup on the line, he was at his best again, turning back the Leafs 3–1 in front of 17,000 ecstatic fans at a packed Chicago Stadium.

It was Chicago's second Stanley Cup championship — and is still the only time a team that finished the regular season below .500 has gone on to win hockey's most famous prize.

Boston beats a bunch of guys named Joe

April 12, 1941

Boston was such a powerhouse that most Red Wing fans had long ago given up on their team's chances of winning the Stanley Cup. Only 8,125 paid admissions, one of the smallest crowds in playoff history, bothered to turn out for the deciding game of the final in Detroit.

The Wings and their followers had been demoralized by a squad acknowledged as one of the strongest ever assembled. Leading the explosive Bruin offence was the famous Kraut Line of Milt Schmidt, Woody Dumart and Bobby Bauer, as well as centre Bill Cowley, who won the scoring race with 62 points. Standing guard in net was Frankie Brimsek, regarded as the outstanding goaltender of the era.

Boston finished first for the fourth season in a row and then knocked off second-place Toronto in a seven-game semi-final. With the score tied 1–1 in the concluding game, Mel "Sudden Death" Hill put the Bruins into the final with another of the clutch goals that had earned him his nickname.

The Wings, who finished in third place and then eliminated the New York Rangers and Chicago Black Hawks, simply weren't in the same class as Boston. "The Red Wings look like a bunch of guys named Joe to me," observed a cocky Mel Hill.

Detroit's offence managed only eight shots against Brimsek in the first two periods of the opener as the Bruins scored early and then coasted to a 3–2 victory. Boston took the next one 2–1. In the third game, Schmidt scored a pair of goals as the Bruins won 4–2.

The Detroit fans had seen enough. One reporter wrote that management must have counted the press, the players and the ushers to raise the attendance total to over 8,000 for the fourth game.

The Wings tried valiantly to put up a fight, but without undue difficulty the Bruins skated to a 3–1 decision to capture their second Stanley Cup in three years.

"Winning that series in four straight was no surprise to us," Milt Schmidt later recalled. "We had a great hockey club at that stage, no doubt about it."

Boston centre Bill Cowley (above) won the scoring title and was also named the league MVP. After game four in Detroit, the Bruins celebrate their second Stanley Cup in three years (right). Coach Cooney Weiland is flanked by all-star defenceman Dit Clapper on the left and Kraut Line pivot Milt Schmidt to the right.

*"We had a great
hockey club, no
doubt about it."*

- *Milt Schmidt*

Toronto's miracle comeback

April 18, 1942

Even many fervent Toronto fans had come to believe that their Leafs were incapable of winning the big games. Toronto had gone to the finals six of the past nine years and each time had come up short.

Now it seemed only a miracle could save them from the same fate again. The Leafs, who had finished 15 points ahead of Detroit in the regular season standings, lost the first three games of the Cup final to the Red Wings. No team had ever come back from such a deficit. Goalie Turk Broda was speaking for most of his demoralized teammates when he said, "Detroit is unbeatable. They can't seem to do anything wrong."

Leaf coach Hap Day decided drastic action was required. He benched scoring ace Gordie Drillon, who had been shut out in the series, as well as slow-footed defenceman Bucko McDonald.

In the dressing room before the start of the fourth match in Detroit, Day shamelessly read aloud a letter from a young girl who, unlike most Leaf fans, still believed her heroes could fight back and win. "We'll win it for the little girl!" winger Billy "the Kid" Taylor said emotionally when Day was finished. "We're not licked yet."

The Leafs triumphed in that match 4–3 and took the next two 9–3 and 3–0 to force a seventh-game showdown in front of 16,218 anxious fans at Maple Leaf Gardens. The score was tied 1–1 in the third period when Red Wing netminder John Mowers charged out of his net to stop a shot. Toronto's Pete Langelle picked up the rebound and put what proved to be the winner into the unguarded cage. Dave "Sweeney" Schriner added an insurance goal as the Leafs went on to celebrate their first championship since 1932.

To this day, Toronto is the only team to lose the first three games of a final series and then come back to capture the Stanley Cup. "I can still see that clock going around in Maple Leaf Gardens at the end of the last game," recalled Toronto captain Syl Apps years later. "I remember thinking, 'Well, they can't beat us now.'"

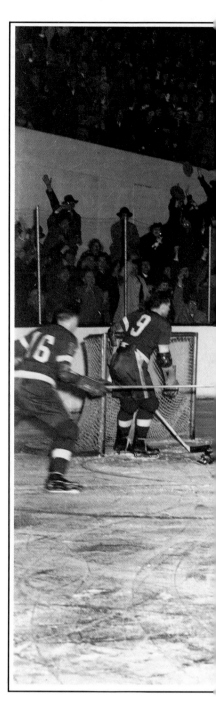

Toronto's Pete Langelle (with arms raised in the centre of the photo) has just fired the puck into the empty Red Wing net to put Toronto ahead 2–1 in game seven. Nowhere to be seen is Detroit goalie John Mowers, who had moved far out of the net to deflect a shot. "The puck happened to bounce ten feet from Mowers," said Langelle, "and I kinda banged at it. Next thing I knew, the red light was on and we were ahead."

*"Detroit is unbeatable.
They can't seem to do
anything wrong."*

- *Turk Broda*

Bill Mosienko's
21-second hat trick

March 23, 1952

"That's one record that'll never be broken," pronounced Chicago coach Ebbie Goodfellow after watching his star right winger Bill Mosienko score a miracle hat trick on the last day of the 1951–52 season.

Mosienko headed into the match against the Rangers at Madison Square Garden with 28 goals to his credit and the hope of scoring a couple more to reach the coveted 30-goal mark. The game itself didn't mean much. Both the fifth-place Rangers and the basement-dwelling Hawks were out of playoff contention. New York took the opportunity to start rookie goaltender Lorne Anderson, who had played just two games in the NHL.

The Rangers controlled play from the start, and by early in the third period had built up a 6–2 lead. Working on Chicago's top line with centre Gus Bodnar and left winger George Gee, Mosienko had been shut out to that point.

Now Goodfellow sent the trio out to take a faceoff. Bodnar won the draw, getting the puck to Mosienko at centre ice. The speedy Mosienko darted around Ranger defenceman Hy Buller and got off a low wrist shot that beat Anderson on the right side. The time was 6:09.

Bodnar, Gee and Mosienko lined up for the faceoff at centre ice, and again Bodnar won the draw, sending the puck to his right winger at the blue line. In full flight, Mosienko sped past Buller and netted his 30th of the season on another low shot that fooled Anderson. The clock read 6:20, just eleven seconds after his first goal.

Again Mosienko lined up with his mates. Streaking into the Ranger zone, he took a pass from Gee, deked to the left and flipped the puck over the shellshocked goaltender. The time was 6:30 and Mosienko had tallied three times in a record 21 seconds.

Remarkably, Mosienko almost had a fourth goal just a few seconds later when he again had Anderson beaten, but missed the post by inches.

Goodfellow finally called Mosienko to the bench. "Bill," he said, "get off the ice, you're in a slump!"

The inspired Black Hawks went on to win the game 7–6.

Mosienko almost had a fourth goal a few seconds later.

At age 30, Mosienko was an 11-year veteran of the NHL wars. His 21-second hat trick bettered the old mark of three goals in one minute and 52 seconds set in 1938 by Carl Liscombe of Detroit.

"Only the Rocket can score a goal like that"

April 8, 1952

It was perhaps the shining moment of Maurice "Rocket" Richard's glorious career.

The overmatched but persistent Boston Bruins had forced Richard's Canadiens to a seventh game in their semi-final round. In the second period, the Rocket cracked his head on the ice after a collision with Bruin defenceman Bill Quackenbush and was carried unconscious to the Montreal Forum clinic. With the score tied 1–1 late in the third period, Richard, a bandage covering a six-stitch gash over his left eye, returned to the Canadiens bench.

"When Richard came from the clinic he told me he was all right," said Canadiens coach Dick Irvin. "But he wasn't just then. He didn't even know the score of the game."

With the series on the line, Irvin couldn't afford to leave the game's greatest clutch performer on the bench. With about four minutes left in the period, Richard was sent back in.

Blood dripping down his face, the Rocket took a pass from teammate Butch Bouchard beside the Canadiens net and then sped past Bruin forward Real Chevrefils toward centre ice. At the Boston blue line, he swept around defenceman Bob Armstrong and then bulled his way through Quackenbush. At the last moment Richard cut in front of goaltender "Sugar" Jim Henry and fired a low shot that caught the corner of the cage.

"The crowd of 14,598 saluted the brilliant play with a roar that shook the building," reported the local *Gazette* the next day. "Programs, coins, newspapers, overshoes and anything that was throwable rained down on the ice."

After the game, while his teammates celebrated around him, Richard sat in the dressing room holding his aching head in his hands. He had only a hazy memory of what had happened. "I heard the crowd yell and by that time I was too dizzy even to see."

Dick Irvin expressed the thoughts of everyone at the Forum when he said, "Only a guy like the Rocket can score a goal like that."

In the second period, Richard was carried unconscious to the Forum clinic.

Dripping blood from a six-stitch gash over his left eye, a still groggy Rocket Richard accepts the congratulations of Boston's "Sugar" Jim Henry after the game in Montreal.

Unbelievable, unbeatable Sawchuk

April 15, 1952

Earlier in the season, Montreal coach Dick Irvin thought that he might possibly have detected a chink in the armour of Terry Sawchuk, Detroit's sensational young goaltender. "If the kid has any weakness, any weakness at all, it's a shoulder-high shot on the right side."

By the time Sawchuk and his teammates were hoisting the Stanley Cup after rolling over Toronto and the Canadiens in the minimum eight playoff games, Irvin was willing to admit that his theory was dead wrong. Sawchuk had stopped high shots and everything else thrown at him in the most spectacular playoff performance ever recorded by a goaltender. In the two series, the 23-year-old had produced four shutouts and given up just five goals for a goals-against average of 0.62, a mark no other goalie has ever come close to matching in the playoffs.

In just his second season, Sawchuk was already regarded as one of the greatest goaltenders in history. He'd won the Calder Trophy as top rookie and then earned the Vezina Trophy in the current campaign. His playoff shutouts equalled the record of four set by Davey Kerr of the New York Rangers in 1937 and Toronto's Frank "Ulcers" McCool in 1945.

Elmer Lach's goal for Montreal in the first period of the second game of the finals was the last that would get by the acrobatic Sawchuk. The powerful Red Wings, who had finished first and were considered one of strongest teams ever, defeated the defending champions by scores of 3–1, 2–1, 3–0 and 3–0.

By the final game in Detroit, the Canadiens had become so frustrated by Sawchuk's larceny that, after one particularly incredible save, trigger-tempered Dickie Moore repeatedly banged his stick on the ice as he skated the length of the rink.

Sawchuk was mobbed by his teammates at the final buzzer. In the dressing room, he was the last to get dressed as reporters crowded around him and wellwishers offered their congratulations.

"I wasn't worried about equalling the playoff shutout record," said the young man who would go on to set the career mark for shutouts. "All I wanted to do was to get this series over with."

The 23-year-old's four playoff shutouts in eight games equalled the record shared by Davey Kerr of the Rangers and Toronto's Frank McCool. But Kerr required nine games and McCool 13 to record their four.

Sawchuk was already regarded as one of the greatest goaltenders in history.

Lach shoots overtime winner for Habs

April 16, 1953

"I never saw it go in! I never saw it go in!" Elmer Lach kept shouting to his celebrating teammates after his overtime goal had earned Montreal its first Stanley Cup since 1946.

"I never saw it either," Boston goaltender "Sugar" Jim Henry said in the losers' dressing room. "He really wound up on that one."

With Montreal leading the series 3–1, tension ran high before the start of the game as the Canadiens sought to clinch on home ice. Police reported that scalpers were asking a record $16 for seats that normally sold for $2.

From the opening faceoff, Boston, who lost the fourth game 7–3, resumed the tenacious checking that had enabled them to defeat first-place Detroit in the semi-finals. As early as the opening period, many in the crowd were predicting the battle would continue into overtime. Lach's winner at 1:22 of extra play was the only goal of the game.

The 13-year veteran could still fly at the age of 35. Leading a Montreal charge, Lach broke across the blue line and fired a shot that bounced off Henry's stick into the corner. Rocket Richard came up with the puck and made a perfect pass back to Lach, who smoked a drive under Henry's elbow into the net.

"I just let the shot go when the puck suddenly came in front of me," said Lach. "I didn't even have time to see the puck go into the net before the Rocket hugged me and knocked me down." Several hundred fans scrambled over the boards to join the celebration. It was several minutes before NHL president Clarence Campbell was able to make his way to centre ice and present the Cup to Canadiens captain Butch Bouchard.

In the Montreal dressing room, coach Dick Irvin said he'd had a hunch that the tall centreman would rise to the occasion.

"You know Elmer came into the room this morning and seemed full of pep, checking over his sticks. I said to him, 'I have a feeling you're going to get a goal tonight,' and he replied, 'You're darn right I am.'"

> *"I never saw it. He really wound up on that one."*
>
> *- Boston goalie "Sugar" Jim Henry*

Lach's overtime winner was his only goal of the 1953 playoffs, and the last the veteran centreman would score in post-season play. Above, Lach comes to the aid of Montreal goaltender Gerry McNeil. Behind the net is his longtime linemate Rocket Richard.

Ted Lindsay mows down the Leafs

March 24, 1956

Intended to intimidate, the death threat made against Ted Lindsay and Gordie Howe before the start of their semi-final match in Toronto had exactly the opposite effect. "You don't scare fellows like that so easily," said Red Wing coach Jimmy Skinner. "The crackpot turned out to be our benefactor because he made Lindsay and Howe mad."

Earlier in the day an anonymous caller, no doubt frustrated by Detroit's 2–0 series lead, had telephoned Toronto newspapers with the message: "Don't worry about Howe and Lindsay tonight. I'm going to shoot them." The police were sufficiently alarmed to assign 12 plainclothes policemen to accompany the Red Wing stars to the rink.

Although Lindsay and Howe initially laughed off the threat, they became increasingly disturbed by the surrounding publicity as the hours ticked down to the opening faceoff. "It annoyed me when my mother got upset after hearing about it on the radio out in Saskatoon," said Howe. "She's almost 70 and already under doctor's care, and when she heard someone was going to shoot me, she was really worried."

The linemates, who had been slumping to this point in the series, responded brilliantly to the mounting pressure. Toronto was leading 4–2 in the third period when Howe and Lindsay went to work. Howe started by firing a 35-footer past Leaf goaltender Harry Lumley to put the Wings within a goal. Then Lindsay snapped a long, low shot into the net to tie it up.

Lindsay won the game and provided the Wings with a commanding 3–0 lead in the series at 4:22 of overtime. The hardnosed veteran known as "Terrible Ted" was perched on the Toronto goalmouth when he took a pass from teammate Bob Goldham and shovelled the puck by Lumley.

As a final gesture of defiance, Lindsay raised his stick toward the crowd and pretended to shoot it like a machinegun.

"If I ever wanted to get two or three goals in my whole life, this was the night," Lindsay said. "That threat made me mad."

Angry, perhaps, but not foolhardy. Howe admitted that when the game was over, "Ted and I hustled off the ice just a little faster than usual."

> "Don't worry about Howe and Lindsay tonight. I'm going to shoot them."
>
> *- Anonymous caller*

After he scored the winning goal, Lindsay raised his stick toward the crowd and pretended to shoot it like a machinegun. Just 5'8" and 160 pounds, "Terrible Ted" was feared and respected as one of the toughest players in the NHL. He led the league in scoring in 1949–50 and was a member of nine All-Star teams during his 17-year career.

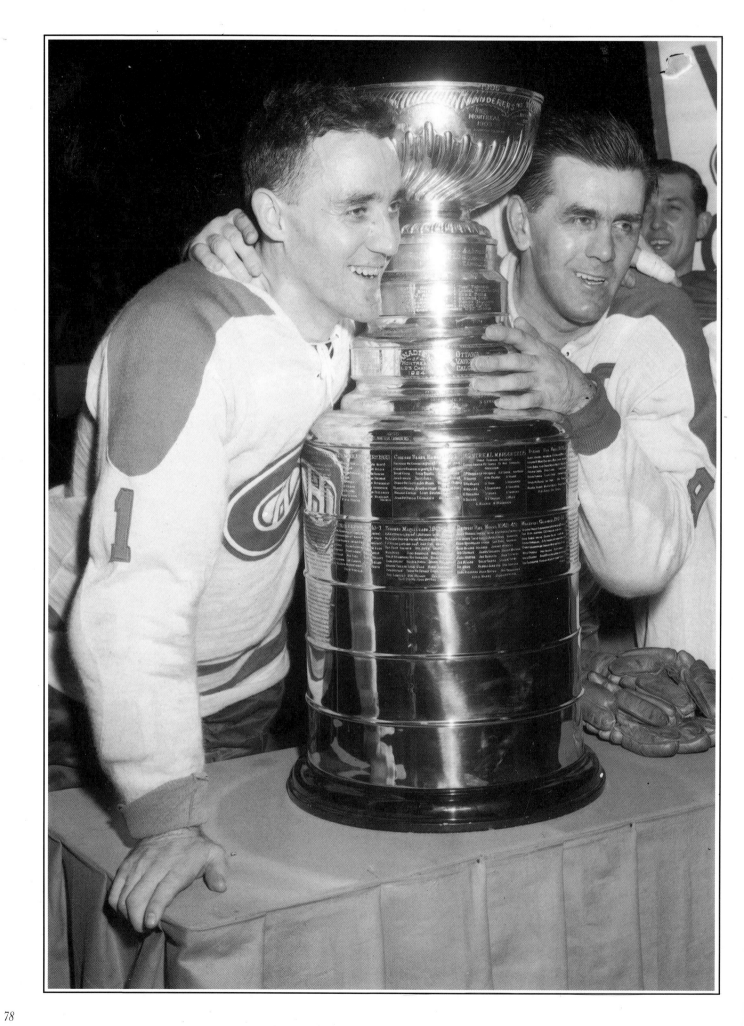

Canadiens win record fifth straight Cup

April 14, 1960

Richard, Beliveau, Geoffrion — Selke had assembled a squadron of superstars.

"This is the greatest hockey team ever assembled," boasted Montreal managing director Frank Selke after the Canadiens rolled to their record fifth straight Stanley Cup.

No other team had ever won more than three Cups in a row. And only one other, the Red Wings of 1952, had duplicated Montreal's recent feat of sweeping through the playoffs in the minimum eight games.

Maurice Richard, Jean Beliveau, Bernie "Boom Boom" Geoffrion, Doug Harvey, Dickie Moore, Henri Richard, Jacques Plante — Selke had assembled a squadron of superstars. Plante won his fifth straight Vezina Trophy as the league's top goaltender. Doug Harvey captured the Norris Trophy as the best defenceman for the fifth time in six years. Beliveau, Geoffrion and Henri Richard all scored 30 or more goals.

For the third year running, Montreal finished the season in first place. Although the Chicago Black Hawks managed to keep the games close in the opening round of the playoffs, the outcome was never in doubt. Plante shut out the Hawks in the final two games.

Montreal's opponents in the finals were Punch Imlach's Toronto Maple Leafs. In an attempt to motivate his men, Imlach dumped $1,250 in dollar bills on the dressing room floor — the difference between a winning and losing share of the playoff money.

It was no good. The Canadiens took the first game 4–2 and the second 2–1. Only the magnificent play of Toronto netminder Johnny Bower kept the scores close.

The highlight of the third game was a goal by 38-year-old Rocket Richard, his 82nd in Cup play and the last of his brilliant career. Richard swept out from behind the Toronto net and blistered a backhander past Bower. The Canadiens won that one 5–2, and then cruised to a 4–0 victory in Toronto to clinch the Stanley Cup.

Afterwards the Canadiens were remarkably subdued, almost as if they'd just played a regular-season game. "Well," smiled future Hall-of-Famer Doug Harvey, "when you win 4–0 and win in four games, and after four Cup titles, you don't get too excited."

Vezina winner Jacques Plante and team captain Rocket Richard pose with the Stanley Cup. Richard, who retired during training camp the following autumn, scored the final playoff goal of his career in game three of the finals when he beat Toronto goalie Johnny Bower with a blistering backhander.

79

Hawks cap the long climb back

April 16, 1961

Chicago coach Rudy Pilous was almost beside himself with joy. "Reggie Fleming's goal did it!" he yelled. "That's when we won it. The goal took the starch out of them and gave us the zip we needed."

For the first time since 1937–38, the Hawks were Stanley Cup champions. The intervening years had been a long, difficult struggle. Chicago missed the playoffs 14 times, and as recently as four years before there had been serious talk that the franchise would be folded.

That's when owner Jim Norris took out his cheque book and began purchasing players from other clubs in a last-ditch attempt to save the team. Of the 18 players on the championship roster, 13 were bought from other squads. But even more important in the Hawks resurgence was the arrival of home-grown young scoring stars Bobby Hull and Stan Mikita.

A tough, aggressive team, Chicago concluded the season in third spot and then needed six games to oust Montreal, the regular season champs and winners of five straight Cups. The Hawks, who had fallen to Montreal in a bitterly contested semi-final series the previous spring, delighted in their victory. "Those guys have laughed at us long enough," said Chicago's brilliant netminder Glenn Hall.

Facing the Hawks in the final were the fourth-place Red Wings, who would also fall in six games. By the concluding match in Detroit, Gordie Howe and his overmatched teammates had run out of steam.

The Wings opened the scoring as they fought desperately to stave off elimination. The lead stood until early in the second period when muscular Reggie Fleming, known more as a brawler than a scorer, stole the puck from Len Lunde and beat Wing netminder Hank Bassen for a short-handed goal.

"That gave everybody a big lift and we just took over from there," said Bobby Hull. The Hawks rolled on to a 5–1 victory.

"Congratulations, Lucky," said Gordie Howe to Rudy Pilous during a visit to the Chicago dressing room.

"Lucky? I'll say I'm lucky," whooped the Hawk coach. "Lucky to have such a great bunch of players and lucky to have an owner who went out and got them for me."

Coach Rudy Pilous guided the Hawks to their first championship since 1938. The Chicago offence was led by 31-goal shooter Bobby Hull. Pierre Pilote anchored the defence, and in net was Glenn Hall, who performed spectacularly throughout the playoffs.

"*Those guys have laughed at us long enough.*"

- *Glenn Hall*

Revitalized Leafs end drought

April 22, 1962

Spoiled by past successes, the Toronto Maple Leafs and their fans had endured what seemed like an endless drought — 11 years without winning a Stanley Cup.

George "Punch" Imlach's crew was a balanced blend of veteran grinders and young skill players such as the high-scoring Frank Mahovlich and smooth centre Dave Keon. The Leafs finished in second spot behind Montreal during the regular season, then took six games to eliminate the fourth-place New York Rangers in the semi-finals. Facing them in the Cup final were the defending champion Chicago Black Hawks, who had dispensed with the Canadiens in six games.

Toronto came out hitting and tried to wear down the usually high-scoring Hawks with their relentless checking.

"They never let us get moving," said Bobby Hull. "You can get a couple of steps on other clubs, but when the Leafs are in form they nail you as soon as you touch the puck. They just checked us to death."

Scrappy left winger Dick Duff was the hero of the sixth and final game, scoring the Cup winner for the Leafs on a power play at 14:14 of the third period. With the score tied 1–1, Duff cut in from the wing and slashed a waist-high shot past goaltender Glenn Hall, who had slid out to try to block the play.

Not a single member of Toronto's eighth championship squad had been around to celebrate the last Cup victory in 1951. Imlach, the brash coach and general manager who was given most of the credit for restoring the team to its former glory, was hired in 1958. Under Imlach's direction, the Maple Leafs had risen from last place in 1958 to play in two of the three previous Stanley Cup finals.

A crowd of 50,000 celebrated in the streets surrounding Toronto's City Hall when hockey's new champions returned home. There would be three more victory parties in the next five years. The drought was over; a new era of Maple Leaf success had begun.

Coach and GM Punch Imlach was the guiding force behind the Toronto resurgence. "I knew when they skated out for the game that they'd come back winners," he said before the Cup victory. "You could sense it." Dick Duff, right, scored the winning goal in the final game.

"*They never let us get moving. They just checked us to death.*"

- Bobby Hull

The almost indestructable Glenn Hall

November 7, 1962

The Chicago goaltender hadn't missed even a minute of game action since the start of the 1955–56 season.

"I guess the fact that I had that string going made me want to play against Boston just that much more," said a disappointed Glenn Hall. "I felt sure I would be able to play."

The 31-year-old Hawk goalkeeper hadn't missed even a minute of game action since the start of the 1955–56 season, when he'd broken in as a regular with the Detroit Red Wings. Before and after his trade to the Black Hawks two seasons later, Hall had played through countless bruises, sprains and cuts to his face. No backstop in history has been as durable as the all-star the Chicago fans called "Mr. Goalie."

The day before the Hawks were to meet the Bruins on home ice, he'd strained a ligament in his lower back while trying to break in a stiff new pair of pads. Despite suffering intense pain, Hall skated out to start the game and extend his streak to an incredible 552 regular-season and playoff matches.

Midway through the first period, Bruin forward Murray Oliver broke across the blue line and fired a shot that slipped between Hall's legs into the net for the first Boston score.

"It was a shot I could have saved, but the pain in my back made me afraid to bend down as far as I should have," Hall said. "I decided it was time to get out of the game."

After 33,135 minutes of continuous play, Hall skated to the bench and told coach Rudy Pilous he was through for the night. Substitute Denis DeJordy finished up as the Hawks and Bruins skated to a 3–3 tie. The injury also forced Hall to sit out the next match against Montreal.

The future Hall-of-Famer explained the work ethic that had kept him going for so long in hockey's most perilous profession. "Sure, there have been times over the years when I wasn't in condition to play. But I feel that I should whenever it's possible. My job is to stop the puck.

"I got to be proud of that string," Hall said sadly. "That was why I started."

Hall's durability was all the more remarkable given that he found his chosen profession so nerve-wracking. He was usually sick to his stomach before a game and sometimes between periods. "I often look at those guys who can whistle and laugh before a game and shake my head," Hall said. "Me? I'm plain miserable before every game."

Espo and the Bruins rewrite the record book

March 11, 1971

Like so many of his goals, Phil Esposito scored his record-breaking 59th of the season while positioned in the area known as the slot, the few square feet directly in front of the enemy goaltender. The tall centre angled his stick and redirected Ted Green's drive from the point into the net past Los Angeles goaltender Denis DeJordy.

The goal, at 7:03 of the first period, shattered the mark established by Bobby Hull in 1968–69, the same year Esposito had himself set the single-season points record of 126, a total he had surpassed the previous night in Oakland.

"To be honest, I felt more pressure two years ago when I was the first to score more than a hundred points in a season," said Esposito in the visitors' dressing room at the Los Angeles Forum. "But I'm glad it's over. With 11 games left after this one, I knew that I'd get the record sooner or later."

Hull had set his mark in a 70-game season. Esposito, a close friend of the Golden Jet when the two played together in Chicago, expressed satisfaction at having scored the goal in his 67th game. "So they won't put an asterisk alongside the record," he said.

Although the game's leading scorer, Esposito was just one cog in a phenomenally potent Boston line-up. Teammate Bobby Orr established a couple of records himself in that night's 7–3 trouncing of the Kings.

Orr's three assists put him at 88 for the season, which broke his record of 87 set the year before, when he became the first defenceman to win a scoring title. His 35th goal raised his own record total of goals by a rearguard.

By the end of the season, the Bruins would own 16 NHL team records and 21 individual marks. Their total of 399 goals was 98 more than any team had scored before. Seven Bruins had 30 or more goals, and ten had 20 or more.

Asked how many he expected to score by the end of the season, Esposito said he'd be satisfied with 65. He concluded the schedule with a league-leading 152 points, including a more than satisfactory 76 goals.

> **By the end of the season, the Bruins would own 16 team scoring records and 21 individual marks.**

Esposito's total of 76 goals by season's end shattered Bobby Hull's old record by 18. Above, Orr and Esposito share the moment in Oakland March 10 after Orr had scored two goals to break his own single-season mark for defenceman and Esposito had equalled Hull's total of 58 goals and bettered his own points record.

Bernie Parent
repeats as playoff MVP

May 27, 1975

By the time the Philadelphia Flyers clinched their second consecutive Stanley Cup, coach Freddy Shero's "system" of short shifts to keep players fresh and of carefully planned offensive thrusts was the talk of hockey, and was given much of the credit for the Flyers success.

"Hockey has been revolutionized by Shero's system," agreed Flyer captain Bobby Clarke after the Buffalo Sabres had been defeated in a six-game final. "But it doesn't hurt to have a Bernie Parent playing goal for you, either."

If not for Parent's magnificence during the regular season and throughout the playoffs, Shero's vaunted system might have been viewed as nothing more than an interesting theory. Parent was the first goaltender in 15 years to win the Vezina Trophy in successive seasons, and then became the first back-to-back winner of the Conn Smythe Trophy as the most valuable performer in the playoffs. Bobby Orr was the only other player who had won it twice, in 1970 and 1972.

At times during the finals Parent resembled a man in a shooting gallery as Gilbert Perreault, Rene Robert, Rick Martin and the other Buffalo sharpshooters broke through to fire almost at will.

"Parent won it for them," said Buffalo goalie Gerry Desjardins after Philadelphia took the opener 4–1. "He came up with the big saves and I didn't. Aside from him it was an even game."

The series was tied after four games, and the momentum seemed to have shifted to the Sabres. Then Parent took charge, repeatedly turning back Buffalo chances to spark a 5–1 Philadelphia victory.

He was also the difference in the Cup clincher in Buffalo, when the Sabres peppered 26 shots at him in the first two periods. Flyers Bob Kelly and Bill Clement scored the game's only goals in the third period as Philadelphia won its second consecutive Stanley Cup.

Even in defeat, the Buffalo fans generously acknowledged Parent's performance, chanting "Bernie! Bernie! Bernie!" when he was again declared the playoff MVP.

Parent took charge, repeatedly turning back Buffalo chances.

Parent had four shutouts in 15 playoff games while posting a goals-against average of 1.89. "The difference tonight was our goaltender," said Flyer captain Bobby Clarke after the final game. "He saves his best games for the playoffs. It was that way last year when we won the Cup from Boston."

Darryl Sittler's ten-point retort

February 7, 1976

In another of the rantings that fans and his players had come to dread, Toronto's controversial owner Harold Ballard made a direct dig at slumping star Darryl Sittler. Ballard told reporters that he "was determined to find a sensational centre" to play between high-scoring wingers Lanny McDonald and Errol Thompson. "We'd set off a time bomb if we had a hell of a centre in there," Ballard said.

One day later Sittler, newly positioned in that supposed trouble spot by coach Red Kelly, delivered the most awesome offensive display in the history of the NHL. He scored six goals and added four assists for a record ten points as the Leafs drubbed the Boston Bruins 11–4 at Maple Leaf Gardens.

"Undoubtedly, Mr. Ballard will figure his little blast inspired me to set the record, but it just isn't that way," said the 25-year-old Leaf captain, who was widely regarded as one of the premier centres in the game. Sittler had raised Ballard's ire by scoring just five times in his previous 17 games.

His ten-point outburst broke the single-game record of eight, held jointly by Rocket Richard and Bert Olmstead. Sittler's six goals fell one short of the all-time record set in 1920 by Joe Malone of the Quebec Bulldogs, but tied the modern-day mark of six held by Syd Howe and Red Berenson.

"It was a night when every time I had the puck, something seemed to happen," Sittler said. "On one goal, I slapped the puck from just inside the Boston blue line and sort of flubbed the shot. But it went between the goalie's legs. My sixth goal was one of those 'when you're hot, you're hot' efforts. I was behind the net, tried a passout towards Thompson and it went in off two skates.

"The thing I'll remember most is the ovation the fans gave me when I got the ninth point. That's something you don't forget."

A beaming, self-satisfied Ballard described Sittler's accomplishment as "a greater feat than Paul Henderson's goal in Russia in 1972."

"Maybe now," replied Sittler, "he won't have to hunt quite so hard for that centre he wants."

> *"Every time I had the puck, something seemed to happen."*
>
> *- Darryl Sittler*

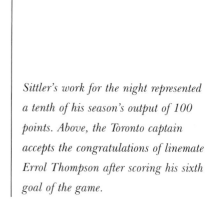

Sittler's work for the night represented a tenth of his season's output of 100 points. Above, the Toronto captain accepts the congratulations of linemate Errol Thompson after scoring his sixth goal of the game.

Lafleur the magnificent

May 10, 1979

Lafleur seemed to be everywhere, constantly pressing the Montreal attack.

Yvon Lambert scored the seventh-game overtime goal that finally subdued Boston and put the Montreal Canadiens into the Stanley Cup finals. But all anyone could talk about was the almost unbelievable performance of Guy Lafleur, the player widely regarded as the best on the planet.

With Boston ahead 3–1 as the third period began at the Montreal Forum, Lafleur got the Canadiens back in the game when he made two beautiful plays to set up goals by Mark Napier and Guy Lapointe.

Napier's score, at 6:10, was a quick 15-footer that he converted after Lafleur swept around the Bruin net and fed him a one-handed pass. Lapointe's goal came at 8:16 on a power play. Lafleur hit him with a perfect pass and Lapointe powered a 50-foot slapshot past Boston goaltender Gilles Gilbert.

Lafleur seemed to be everywhere, constantly pressing the Montreal attack. A team official later said he had played 46 minutes of a 69-minute game.

"I don't ever remember playing that much," Lafleur said. "But what difference does it make? We had to do everything possible to beat a team that just wouldn't give up. I wasn't the only one who worked a little overtime."

Boston's Rick Middleton scored his second goal of the game to put the Bruins back in front. Then, at 17:26, Boston was given the most famous penalty in playoff history — two minutes for having too many men on the ice.

Lafleur went to work again. He passed the puck to Jacques Lemaire, who fed it back to him as he streaked over the blue line, his stick already raised to shoot. Lafleur's blast was behind Gilbert before he could make a move.

At 9:33 of overtime, Yvon Lambert converted a pass from Mario Tremblay to put Montreal in the finals against the New York Rangers, a series Lafleur and company would win in five games to claim their fourth consecutive Stanley Cup.

"What more could we have possibly done to win?" asked heartbroken Boston defenceman Brad Park. "Give the Canadiens, and especially Guy Lafleur, credit. They just didn't quit."

Lafleur's tying goal came on the power play after Don Cherry's Bruins were penalized for having too many men on the ice. "That was my fault," said a crestfallen Cherry. "When you get caught with too many on the ice at that stage of the game, it's the coach's fault."

Philly's inconvenient unbeaten streak

January 7, 1980

To hear Philadelphia coach Pat Quinn tell it, going so many games without a loss was a nuisance he could quite happily have done without.

"I don't feel bad that it's over," said Quinn when the longest unbeaten streak in the history of North American professional sports finally ended at 35 games. "It was exciting and it certainly created a lot of interest. But, you know, in some ways it impeded what we were trying to do."

The Flyers were in the midst of a rebuilding program, with a lineup dominated by veteran forwards coming off mediocre seasons, young defencemen given to sloppy mistakes, and suspect goaltending. Quinn expected to spend at least the first two or three months of the campaign working on fundamentals and trying to determine which players fit into his long-range plans.

But when the Flyers kept on winning, Quinn was naturally reluctant to tamper with success. The streak started in the third game of the season with a victory over Toronto. By the time they passed the old record of 28 games without a loss set by Montreal in 1977–78, the team was being followed by a small army of newspaper reporters and television crews. In December, the Flyers shattered the all-pro mark of 33 consecutive games held by basketball's Los Angeles Lakers.

The end finally came at the hands of the Minnesota North Stars. Playing before a record crowd at the Metropolitan Sports Center in Bloomington, the Stars spotted Philadelphia the first goal and then roared back for a 7–1 triumph.

"I told them I was proud of them," said Quinn after his club's streak was stopped at 25 wins and ten ties. "We only lost a hockey game, nothing more."

Now Quinn had to hurry up and do the teaching he had put on hold during the record run. The Flyers went on to finish atop the overall standings and then extended the New York Islanders to six games before succumbing in the Stanley Cup finals.

The coach was left to wonder what might have been if only his team hadn't won so darned many games early in the season.

Led by 11-year veteran Bobby Clarke (16), the Flyers put together the longest winning streak in the history of North American professional sports. Philadelphia went on to top the standings for the first time since their Stanley Cup–winning year of 1974–75.

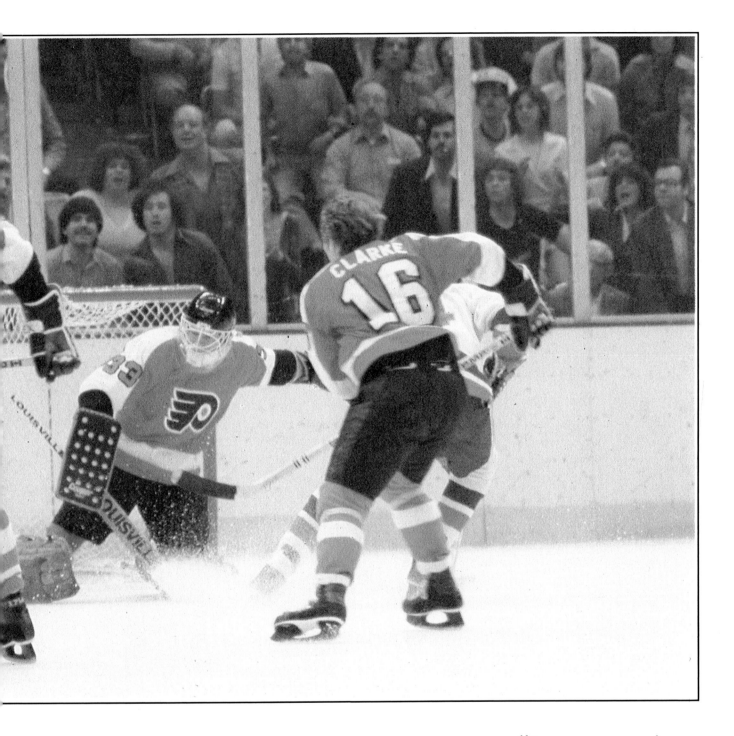

*"In some ways it
impeded what we
were trying to do."*

- Pat Quinn

Tonelli pulls champs back from brink

April 13, 1982

It was a spring full of surprises. Montreal, Edmonton and Minnesota, all of whom easily won their divisions, had been ousted in the first round of the playoffs. And now the mighty New York Islanders, two-time defending Stanley Cup champions, were on the verge of suffering one of the most stunning upsets in the history of post-season play.

After barely scraping into the playoffs, the Pittsburgh Penguins forced the Islanders to a decisive fifth game in their best-of-five opening-round series. Thanks mostly to the sensational play of their goalkeeper, Michel Dion, who would handle 46 shots before the night was through, the Pens clung stubbornly to a 3–1 lead after two periods.

"Dion was absolutely super," praised his Islander counterpart, Billy Smith. "It was one of the most outstanding jobs I've ever seen a goalie turn in."

Although the Islanders constantly pressed the attack, they still trailed by two goals with less than six minutes left in the third period. Dion was finally beaten by Mike McEwen on a power play at 14:33. Just over three minutes later, rugged winger John Tonelli whipped a puck past the Pittsburgh goalie to even the score.

As the organist at Nassau Coliseum repeatedly pounded out the Islanders theme song, "We Are the Champions," the battle continued into overtime. Following spectacular saves by both goalies, the end came after six minutes and 19 seconds of play.

Tonelli, who at age 25 had blossomed into a 35-goal sniper, was hauled down from behind on a breakaway and knocked off the puck. He fought tenaciously to regain possession and then passed off to Bob Nystrom, who fired at the net. Tonelli picked up the rebound and flipped it in over a sprawling Dion.

"My legs, everything went out on me," said an exhausted Tonelli. "I could hardly raise my stick."

The Islanders comeback demonstrated the talent and determination that had already helped them win two Cups, and would bring them a third in the weeks ahead. But, as Tonelli was happy to admit, the surprising Penguins had scared one of hockey's greatest teams "half to death."

John Tonelli (centre) has just scored the overtime goal that saved the two-time defending Stanley Cup champions from elimination at the hands of the Pittsburgh Penguins. Joining in the celebration are Bob Nystrom (lying on the ice) and Butch Goring.

The Pittsburgh Penguins clung stubbornly to a 3–1 lead after two periods.

Coffey outscores Orr

The record breaker came after a spectacular rink-long dash that reminded spectators of Bobby Orr, the man whose single-season mark of 46 goals by a defenceman had just been eclipsed.

Edmonton's Paul Coffey picked up the puck behind his own net and started up the ice. At the Vancouver blue line, he split between two Canuck defenders and outskated another to the net. Coffey hesitated a moment as goaltender Wendell Young dropped to the ice, then shot the puck into the twine on the far side of the net.

"It was as if he said, 'I may as well do it the right way,'" said an admiring Glen Sather, the Oilers coach and general manager, after the 8–4 win in Edmonton.

Earlier in the game, Coffey, 24, had tied Orr's record on a bank shot that glanced off Canuck defenceman Doug Lidster into the net. "To get a lucky one gave me a jump for the second one," Coffey said. "I shouldn't say I knew, but I had a good feeling before the end of the night I'd get the 47th. As soon as I got the first one, I felt I had 1,000 pounds removed from my back."

Entering the season, Coffey never imagined he'd break Orr's record, which had stood since 1974–75. "I thought it was impossible until about a month and a half ago when people mentioned it and I began to feel the pressure."

Orr wasn't among the capacity crowd of 17,498 at Northlands Coliseum who cheered Coffey's achievement, but he did send a telegram of congratulations. "I'm pleased that a person of your calibre is succeeding me in the record books," it read. Orr also praised the young star as one of hockey's best off-ice ambassadors.

With two games left to play in the schedule, Coffey was just two points shy of matching Orr's single-season points mark of 139 set in 1970–71. Although he scored another goal, the record remained the property of the legend Coffey saluted as "the greatest defenceman ever."

> *"I shouldn't say I knew, but I had a good feeling I'd get the 47th."*
>
> *- Paul Coffey*

Following his record-setting season, Coffey was awarded the Norris Trophy as the NHL's outstanding defenceman for the second straight year.

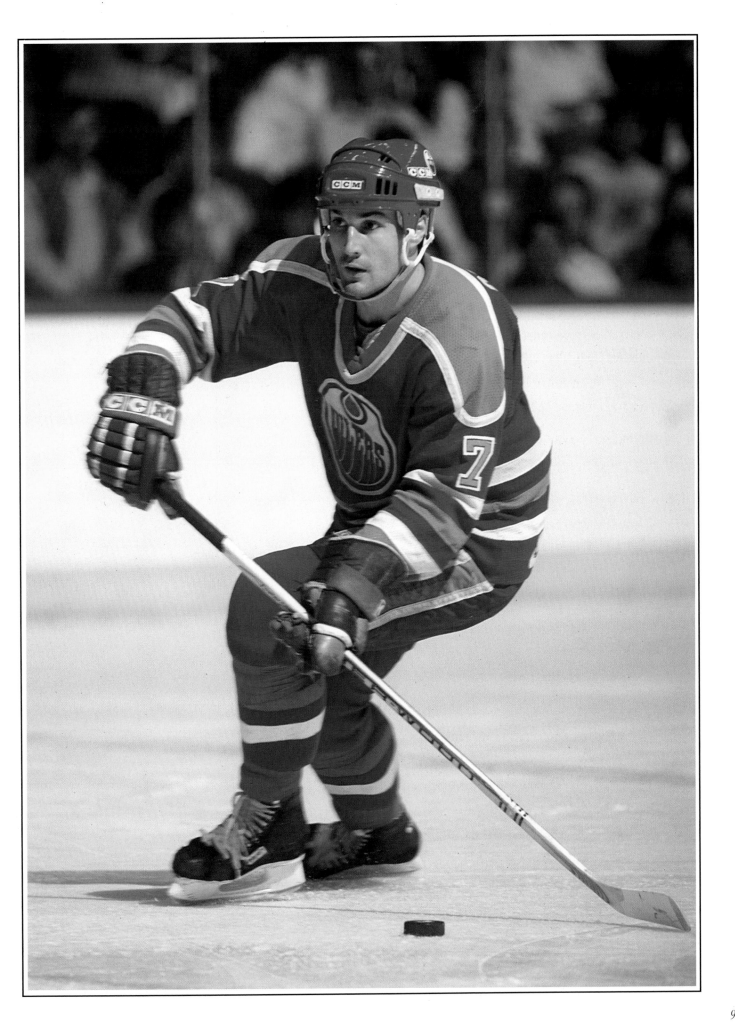

Habs win record 23rd championship

May 24, 1986

"Everyone was scared at the end," admitted Montreal's rookie goaltender Patrick Roy. "I've never been so scared in my life," agreed young forward Mike McPhee.

Fear was not an emotion that such illustrious predecessors as Howie Morenz and Rocket Richard would ever have acknowledged. But the Canadiens who subdued the Calgary Flames to become the first North American professional sports team to win 23 championships (breaking a tie with baseball's New York Yankees) were unlike the powerhouse Montreal squads that had ruled hockey before them. No one expected these guys to win.

Montreal introduced eight rookies — including Roy, Brian Skrudland, Claude Lemieux and Stephane Richer — during a regular season that saw them finish seventh overall. Yet somehow, by the start of the playoffs, the mix of youngsters and veterans had blended into a unit with unexpected balance and poise.

Larry Robinson anchored the defence. Providing leadership up front were Bob Gainey and Bobby Smith. Although the Canadiens didn't score a lot of goals, they always seemed to produce when it was needed most.

The Cup was up for grabs after Calgary eliminated the defending-champion Edmonton Oilers in the second round of the playoffs. Backed by the brilliant goaltending of Roy, who won the Conn Smythe Trophy as the most valuable playoff performer, Montreal defeated the Whalers, Bruins and Rangers to reach the finals.

Calgary won the opener on home ice. Then a combination of tight checking and young legs wore down the Flames as the Canadiens won four straight to clinch the Cup.

It was the final minutes of the last game that set the Canadiens nerves on edge. Montreal was ahead 4–1 and seemingly cruising to victory when Calgary scored two quick goals. With just seconds remaining on the clock, Roy was forced to make a spectacular last save against Jamie Macoun to preserve the win.

Even captain Bob Gainey, a grizzled veteran of four previous Montreal championships, confessed to being "really scared in the last minute."

Morenz and Richard might have cringed. But for the winningest team in pro sports, the result was still the same.

> **The Canadiens were unlike the powerhouse Montreal squads that had ruled hockey before them. No one expected these guys to win.**

Conn Smythe Trophy winner Patrick Roy celebrates Montreal's record-setting victory over the Flames in Calgary. The 20-year-old goaltender was one of eight rookies on the Canadiens roster.

Gretzky shatters Howe's all-time points mark

October 15, 1989

To Edmonton fans, it seemed almost predestined that Wayne Gretzky would break Gordie Howe's all-time points record in the city of his greatest accomplishments. A wildly excited capacity crowd of 17,503 filled Northlands Coliseum — known locally as the House That Gretzky Built — to cheer on the 28-year-old legend who now wore a Los Angeles uniform, but still owned their hearts.

Gretzky tied Howe's mark of 1,850 points in the first period when he assisted on a goal by Bernie Nicholls. The record breaker came at 19:07 of the third frame with the Kings trailing 4–3. Gretzky pounced on a pass from teammate Dave Taylor and flipped a backhander past Oilers goaltender Bill Ranford.

Chants of "Gretz-ky! Gretz-ky! Gretz-ky!" thundered through the arena as the game was interrupted for a ceremony at centre ice. Flanked by his wife Janet and his father Walter, Gretzky accepted the congratulations of Gordie Howe and was hugged by Mark Messier, the Oilers captain and a close friend. Messier presented him with a diamond bracelet containing 1.851 carats, spelling out "1,851." League president John Ziegler gave Gretzky a commemorative silver tray.

"Everything I have in life, I owe to the game of hockey," Gretzky nervously addressed the crowd. "Thank you very much."

Play was resumed and the game went into overtime. At 3:24 of extra play, Gretzky spun around the net and swept the puck past Ranford for the winning goal.

Gretzky's career tally now stood at 642 goals and 1,210 assists in 780 games over 11 seasons. In an NHL career that spanned 26 seasons, Howe, whom Gretzky had idolized since childhood, scored 801 goals and 1,049 assists in 1,767 games.

As Gretzky held court for reporters in the Kings dressing room, Gordie Howe, who had retired at age 52 eight seasons before, was jokingly asked if he might consider a comeback in an attempt to get the record back.

"Naw," Howe said after a pause, "I'd never catch up anyway. Besides, Wayne is such an outstanding individual that it's an honour to hand the record over to him."

> *"Everything I have in life, I owe to the game of hockey."*
>
> *- Wayne Gretzky*

Wayne Gretzky, Kings owner Bruce McNall, Janet Jones Gretzky and Gordie Howe during the on-ice ceremony after No. 99 broke the all-time points mark. "Someone asked me what I thought about replacing Gordie Howe and I just had to laugh," Gretzky had said earlier. "Me replacing Gordie? That's really funny! There's one Gordie Howe. That's all there is to that."

Gartner heads exclusive 30-goal club

March 26, 1994

Like most hockey players, Toronto's Mike Gartner was used to skating in the large shadow cast by Wayne Gretzky. He finished second to No. 99 in balloting for Rookie of the Year when the two broke into the World Hockey Association in 1978. And if Gretzky hadn't come down with a bad back and scored just 16 goals in the 1992–93 season, Gartner would almost certainly have had to accept a junior partner's share of the spotlight for his most recent accomplishment.

"I'm sure Wayne would have done it too if he hadn't been injured last year," Gartner acknowledged after scoring two goals against the Quebec Nordiques for his record 15th consecutive 30-goal season, two more than Gretzky, Phil Esposito and Bobby Hull. He now also topped the career list for most 30-goal campaigns, ahead of Gretzky, Gordie Howe and Marcel Dionne, who shared second place with 14.

Gartner had been a model of consistency since breaking into the NHL with the Washington Capitals the season following his WHA debut. While playing for four teams over 14 seasons, he missed only 35 games, and had never scored fewer than 33 goals. His total of 613 career scores placed him fifth in the all-time ranking.

"Consistency is something I've always strived for," said Gartner, who had been acquired by Toronto from the New York Rangers the week before. "I want the coach to know what to expect from me every game."

The right winger scored his 29th goal of the season — and first as a Maple Leaf — when he rushed down his wing and slapped a shot through the legs of Quebec goaltender Stephane Fiset. His record 30th was put into an empty net with 2:42 left in the game when the Nordiques tried in vain to come back from a two-goal deficit.

Still one of the fastest skaters in the league at the age of 34, Gartner foresaw much more of the same type of production ahead. "I don't feel any different than I did ten years ago," he said. "They think I'll be able to do this for another two, three or four years, and that's what I plan on doing."

> "*They think I'll be able to do this for another two, three or four years, and that's what I plan on doing.*"
>
> *– Mike Gartner*

Gartner's most productive campaign was with the Washington Capitals in 1984–85, when the right winger scored 50 goals with 52 assists. He notched 49 goals while skating for the New York Rangers in 1990–91, and twice had 48 for the Capitals.

"He loved to play hockey more than anyone ever loved anything and when he realized he would never play again, he couldn't live with it. I think Howie died of a broken heart."

- Aurel Joliat speaking
of Howie Morenz

Feuds, tragedies, firsts and flukes

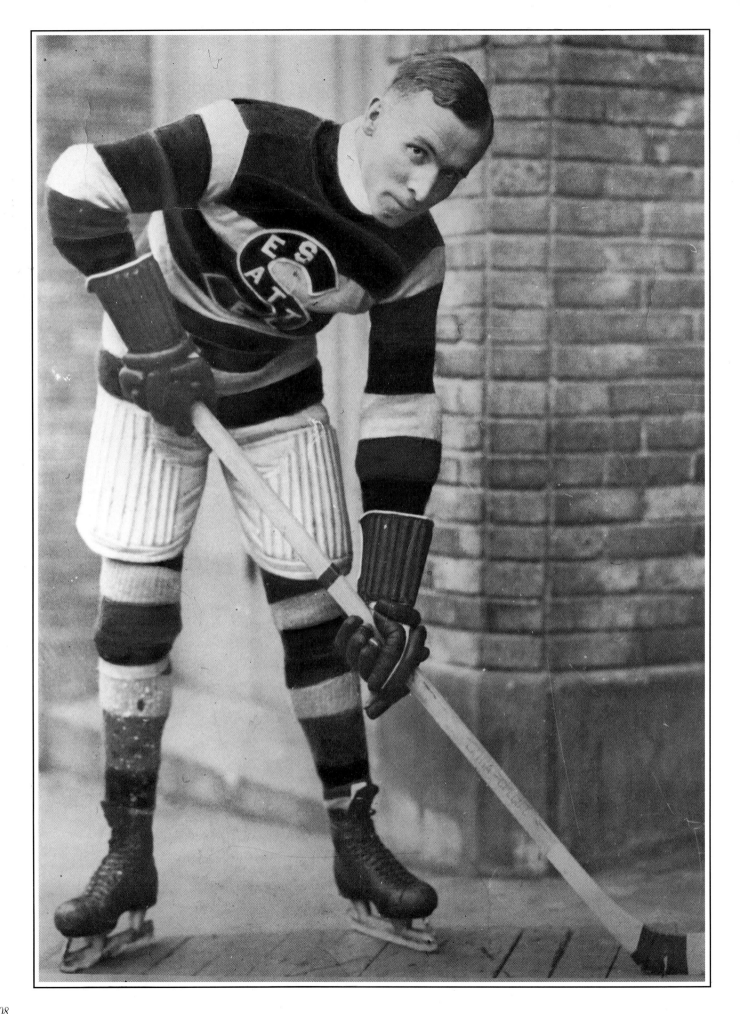

Seattle takes the Cup south of the border

In the fourth and final match, Seattle humiliated the Canadiens 9–1.

In March 1917 the Montreal Canadiens made the long trek west to defend their Stanley Cup title against the Seattle Metropolitans, champions of the Pacific Coast Hockey Association. For the first time a Cup game would be played outside of Canada.

Seattle, in only its second season of operation, had a formidable lineup that included acquired scoring stars Frank Foyston and Bernie Morris. Bold and clever on the attack, although somewhat awkward-looking with his choppy skating stride, Foyston scored 36 goals in the 24-game schedule and was named the best all-round player in the PCHA by a panel of sportwriters. The smooth-skating Morris was perhaps an even more dangerous attacker. He finished second in the scoring race with 37 goals, and would dominate against Montreal as few players have in a series before or since.

Future Hall-of-Famer Frank Foyston (left) and high-scoring Bernie Morris led the Metropolitans to a lopsided victory over the Montreal Canadiens. "You missed one of the all-time greats if you never saw Frank Foyston perform with a hockey stick," said the Seattle Post-Intelligencer *many years later. "He wielded it like Fritz Kreisler his bow, Willie Mays his bat and Arnold Palmer his two-iron."*

Led by forward stars "Newsy" Lalonde and Didier "Cannonball" Pitre, as well as the great goaltender Georges Vezina, Montreal won the opener of the best-of-five series 8–4. Pitre fired his bullet shots past Seattle goaltender Hap Holmes four times, and Morris retaliated with three for the Metropolitans.

Seattle evened the series with a 6–1 victory in the second game as Foyston scored a hat trick and Morris added two more. By the third match the Metropolitans had taken complete control. The slick Morris notched another hat trick and Foyston added a single tally in a 4–1 decision.

In the fourth and final match, Seattle humiliated the Canadiens 9–1. "But the game was really a whitewash for the eastern champions," recounted the *Vancouver Daily Sun*. "They were outclassed in every department of the play."

Bernie Morris put in a remarkable performance, "jockeying the Canadiens defence out of line on numerous occasions" to score six times and raise his tally to 14 for the series. Foyston chipped in with two.

"We were outclassed," admitted Montreal manager George Kennedy, "and you can say for me that Seattle deserved to win." Although every member of the Metropolitans was a Canadian, for the first time the Stanley Cup would reside south of the border.

First All-Stars skate for Ace Bailey

February 14, 1934

For a tense moment the crowd held its breath. Then a smiling Ace Bailey clasped the hand of Eddie Shore, the Boston star who had brutally ended his playing career, and Toronto's Maple Leaf Gardens erupted in a prolonged ovation.

The first All-Star game in NHL history raised more than $20,000 on behalf of the former right winger who had been a Toronto favourite since he broke into the league in 1926. In 1928–29 Irving "Ace" Bailey became the first Leaf to win a scoring championship, netting 22 goals and 10 assists during the 44-game season.

Bailey's dramatic meeting with Shore at centre ice during the opening ceremonies was their first since the night of December 12, 1933, when the slender Leaf veteran had lain on the ice in Boston with a fractured skull.

Shore, known as the "Edmonton Express" for his belligerent style of play, attacked Bailey after being tripped by the Leafs King Clancy. Once back on his feet, Shore mistook Bailey for Clancy and drove into him from behind with all his force. Bailey did a backward flip and crashed head-first onto the ice.

Doctors operated through the night. Things looked so grim that Boston's morning papers printed his death notice. It was almost two weeks before doctors were certain that Bailey would pull through. But, at age 30, his playing days were over.

Bailey at first threatened to sue both Shore and the Bruins. Then the All-Star benefit was suggested as a compromise. The league's best players were invited to play the Leafs in an exhibition in Toronto with all proceeds put into a fund for Bailey.

By the night of the benefit Shore had made a public apology and served a 16-game suspension. Many felt that Shore, who had spent his time off vacationing in Bermuda, was treated too leniently.

Bailey's show of forgiveness during the benefit's opening ceremonies put the issue to rest. The crowd of 14,074 settled back to watch as the Leafs beat history's first squad of All-Stars 7–3.

Bailey's meeting with Shore was the first since the Boston star had brutally ended his playing career.

Eddie Shore and Ace Bailey pose for the cameras (top right) before the start of hockey's first All-Star game. "I know it was an accident," said Bailey, exonerating Shore. The Leafs wore blue uniforms with the word "ACE" across the chest; the All-Stars were outfitted in orange with black trim.

"ACE" BAILEY BENEFIT GAME, TORONTO, FEB 14, 1934, NATIONAL LEAGUE ALL-STARS VERSUS TORONTO MAPLE LEAFS

R.HEWITSON   B. O'BRIEN   H. KILREA   E. SHORE   C.CONACHER   W. COOK   C. SANDS   L. CONACHER   A. BLAIR   A. SHIELDS   H.COTTON   N.STEWART   H.JACKSON   C.JOHNSON   T. DALY   M. RODDEN

F. SELKE   M. DUTTON   C. DAY   R. SMITH   L. DANDURAND   L. PATRICK   F. CALDER   C. SMYTHE   D. IRVIN   H. MORENZ   F. CLANCY   J. WARD

G. HAINSWORTH   K. DORATY   L. AURIE   W. THOMS   N. HIMES   A. LEVINSKY   F. FINNIGAN   R. HORNER   B. BOLL   H. LEWIS   J. PRIMEAU   A. JOLIAT   C. GARDINER

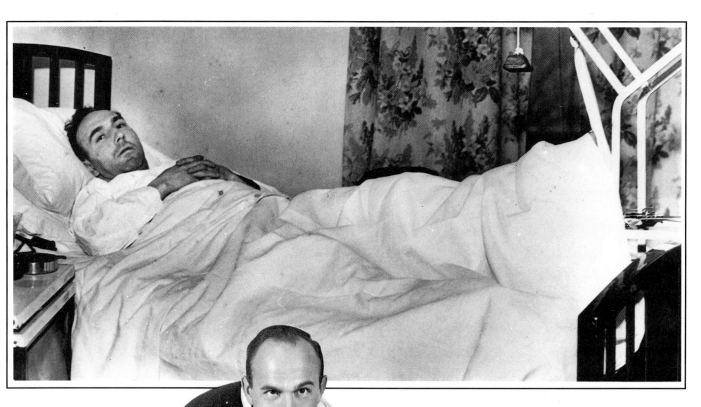

In 550 NHL games, Morenz scored 270 goals, won the scoring title twice and was named the league MVP three times. While recuperating in the hospital (above), the "Stratford Streak" at first spoke bravely about a comeback. But friends said his spirit broke once he realized his career was over.

Death of Howie Morenz shocks hockey world

> *"I think Howie died of a broken heart."*
>
> *- Aurel Joliat*

Montrealers who were there say the city has never been so shaken by a single event, or demonstrated its love so effusively for any other man.

An estimated 250,000 mourners watched the funeral procession for Howie Morenz wind its way toward the Montreal Forum. As four of his teammates formed a guard of honour, Morenz's body was placed at centre ice, surrounded by five truckloads of flowers.

In the four hours before the start of the service, some 50,000 mourners, many weeping openly, filed past the coffin. What made Morenz's passing so difficult for his fans to accept was its suddenness. No one had had time to prepare for the loss of hockey's most famous hero.

Morenz had been a star from the moment he joined the Montreal Canadiens in 1923. Called the "Stratford Streak" after his hometown and for his blinding speed, he led the Habs to three Stanley Cups, and was named the league's most valuable player three times.

"Howie was the greatest player I ever saw," said Toronto Maple Leaf star Frank "King" Clancy. "He could get to top speed in one stride...and he shot the puck as hard as any man ever did."

As the years passed Morenz began to slow down. He was traded to Chicago in 1934, then spent the next season with the New York Rangers. But both he and the Montreal fans had been overjoyed when the Canadiens reacquired him before the start of the current season.

He was 34 when he played his last game January 28, 1937, against Chicago at the Forum. On a rush into the Hawk zone, Morenz crashed into the boards, breaking his ankle and four bones in his leg.

In the hospital, Morenz at first talked bravely about a comeback. But he soon fell into a deep depression. On March 8 he died in his sleep from what the doctors described as a coronary embolism.

Many of his friends thought differently. "He loved to play hockey more than anyone ever loved anything and when he realized that he would never play again, he couldn't live with it," said his linemate Aurel Joliat. "I think Howie died of a broken heart."

"Sudden Death" Mel Hill's curse of success

March 21, 23, April 2, 1939

It's not easy carrying around a reputation as one of the game's greatest clutch performers. Just ask "Sudden Death" Mel Hill, on whose shoulders fame and its burdens settled in 1939 when he scored three overtime goals for Boston in a dramatic semi-final series against the New York Rangers.

"It seemed like I was expected to be the hero in every playoff game from that moment on," Hill lamented years later to *The Hockey News*. "I was a basic, unspectacular player who usually performed well when it counted, but I just happened to get super-hot in that series with New York."

Hill was then a rookie left winger with a powerful Boston squad that finished in first place. He contributed just ten goals during the regular season.

Destiny began its course in the opener against New York. Tied 1–1 at the end of regulation time, the game dragged on late into a third overtime period. It was 1:10 a.m. when Hill took a pass from Bill Cowley and beat Ranger goaltender Davey Kerr with a high shot to end the game.

"I scored on Kerr again the following night in overtime and we took a 2–0 lead over New York," remembered Hill.

Boston also won the next game, but then the Rangers roared back with three straight victories to force a seventh-game showdown at the Boston Garden.

With the score tied 1–1, the teams fought into a tension-packed overtime that, just as in the first game, extended on into a third period. And again, it was Mel Hill who assumed the hero's role.

Cowley fed him a pass that put him all alone in front of Ranger goaltender Bert Gardiner. "I held the puck for a second then flipped it up into the net on the short side," Hill recounted.

Having by now been cursed by a Boston writer with the moniker "Sudden Death," Hill continued to play well as the Bruins defeated Toronto in a five-game final to take the Stanley Cup.

"The name 'Sudden Death' was easier to live with after I retired," joked an elderly Hill. "But at my current age, it has some scary implications."

> *"It seemed like I was expected to be the hero in every playoff game from that moment on."*
>
> *- Mel Hill*

Bruins Mel Hill (11) and Flash Hollett celebrate another playoff victory. Boston management rewarded Hill with a bonus of $1,000 for his overtime heroics and he received another $2,000 in playoff money to double his rookie-year salary of $3,000.

*"If I didn't know what
I was going to do, how
could the goaltender?"*

- Rocket Richard

Rocket Richard notches 50 in 50

Richard is pictured with Montreal coach Dick Irvin. The Rocket claimed that he drew inspiration from the adoration of the Montreal fans. "I played for myself, the team and the fans," he said. "I don't think I would have done as well anywhere else — in fact, I would have refused to play anywhere else — because of the rapport I had with the fans."

"When I got my 50 goals, I had to average a goal a game and that took some doing, I can tell you," recalled Maurice "Rocket" Richard several decades after he became the first sniper to reach the 50-goal plateau. "Not only is the schedule longer now, the teams are weaker because of expansion, and it is easier to score goals."

Rocket was 23 and already established as a rising star when the 1944–45 campaign opened. After scoring 32 times the previous season, he had turned in his famous five-goal effort in a playoff game against Toronto.

Most of Richard's goals came in bunches, which helped him maintain a goal-a-game pace right from the start of the 50-game schedule. He scored two or more goals ten times. One night he equalled his performance of the previous spring by notching five in a game against the Red Wings.

On February 25 in Montreal, Richard took a pass from linemate Toe Blake and snapped a wrist shot past Toronto netminder Frank McCool for his 45th goal of the season, which broke the old mark of 44 set by Joe Malone of the Canadiens in 1917–18. As Blake dived into the net to retrieve the souvenir, the Forum shook with applause. Malone himself later presented the puck to Richard in a special ceremony.

Even though he now owned the record, Richard was determined to reach 50. He had 49 goals as the Canadiens met the Hawks on home ice in the second-to-last match of the season. Desperate to score one more for the Montreal fans, Richard's best opportunity came late in the third period when he was awarded a penalty shot after being hauled down from behind on a breakaway. But the Rocket missed, and his 50th would have to wait until the next night, March 18, in Boston.

Looking back, Richard felt almost sorry for the goalies he faced in those days. "I never knew what I was going to do when I went in until I did it," he said. "If the goaler moved I'd make the play, if he didn't I'd go for one of the corners. If I didn't know what I was going to do, how could the goaltender?"

Toronto captain Ted Kennedy accepts the Cup from league president Clarence Campbell. Known as one of the greatest money players in the history of the game, Leaf goalie Turk Broda (left) limited the usually high-scoring Red Wings to just five goals in the four-game final.

Leafs score first Cup hat-trick

April 16, 1949

"I don't know why you guys are so excited at winning the Stanley Cup. We do it every year."

- Leaf trainer Tim Daly

Toronto's managing director Conn Smythe burst into the Leaf dressing room. "You did it!" he shouted. The Leafs had just become the first NHL team to win the Stanley Cup three years in a row.

In sweeping Detroit in four straight games in the finals, Smythe's Maple Leafs had established a couple of other records as well. Toronto became the first fourth-place club to capture the big prize, and they had now won an unparalleled nine consecutive games in Cup finals, a string that dated back to the final game of the 1947 playoffs.

Netminder Turk Broda, who limited the usually high-scoring Red Wings to just five goals, was asked to make a short speech during the dressing room celebrations in Toronto.

"I want to thank the boys..." he began, then stopped, seemingly flustered.

"For making me a great goaltender," suggested a laughing Smythe.

"Yes," agreed Broda to applause. "For making me a great goaltender."

Broda played well against Detroit, but the Red Wings hadn't been able to muster their usual firepower. After finishing first during the regular season, Detroit had battled Montreal through a gruelling seven-game semi-final. The Leafs, meanwhile, were rested and ready to ambush the exhausted Red Wings after requiring only five games to dispense with the Boston Bruins.

Led by recent minor-league call-up Sid Smith, who scored three goals, and Max Bentley, who potted two, the Leafs won by scores of 3–2, 3–1, 3–1 and 3–1. Toronto's defence even managed to shut out Gordie Howe, who had put eight into the net against Montreal.

"We just couldn't score goals," said Detroit general manager Jack Adams, pacing the floor of the losers' dressing room. "We lost the Cup in that seven-game semi-final with Montreal."

Meanwhile, the Toronto celebration continued unabated. At one point the merrymaking was interrupted by the loud voice of the Leafs veteran trainer, Tim Daly.

"I don't know why you guys are so excited at winning the Stanley Cup," he said straight-faced. "We do it every year."

Howe near death after playoff mishap

The course of hockey history came perilously close to being rewritten when Gordie Howe crashed face-first into the boards late in the opening game of Detroit's semi-final with Toronto. Just three days shy of his 22nd birthday, Howe lay motionless on the ice of the Olympia, his worried teammates crouched over him. For the next several hours he hovered near death. And in the days to come there was concern that he might never play again.

With the Leafs closing in on a 5–0 victory, Toronto's Ted Kennedy had stopped abruptly as Howe moved in to check him. Howe stumbled, and then smashed into the boards. No one was certain whether he had made contact with Kennedy or not.

Still unconcious, Howe was rushed to hospital. His nose and cheekbone were broken, his eyeball was scratched, and his skull was severely fractured. Examining doctors feared possible brain damage.

"I did wake and realized something was going on," Howe said. "Then they started shaving my head and I thought, 'Hell, no!' Then I remember the drilling to relieve the pressure."

Back at the Olympia, Howe's enraged teammates accused Kennedy of butt-ending him, a charge Kennedy, one of the game's most gentlemanly players, denied. Sid Abel received a penalty for swinging his stick at Kennedy once play resumed. From that point on, the series became one of the most vicious ever waged, with Detroit finally winning in seven games.

It was several days before doctors were able to assure Howe that he would play again. On April 23, he was permitted to attend the seventh game of the Stanley Cup finals between the Wings and New York Rangers in Detroit. Wearing a hat over his shaved head, Howe watched from a seat near the Red Wing bench as Pete Babando scored the winner for Detroit in the second overtime period.

As the Red Wings celebrated, the crowd began chanting "We want Howe! We want Howe!" The young star walked onto the ice as the fans let up a mighty roar. Handed the Cup, Howe raised it above his head and then led a parade of his teammates to the Detroit dressing room.

His skull was severely fractured. Doctors feared possible brain damage.

Gordie Howe is carried off the ice at the Detroit Olympia by his concerned teammates (above). While recuperating in hospital, the young Red Wing star, who had scored 35 goals during the regular season, received hundreds of letters and get-well cards from his fans.

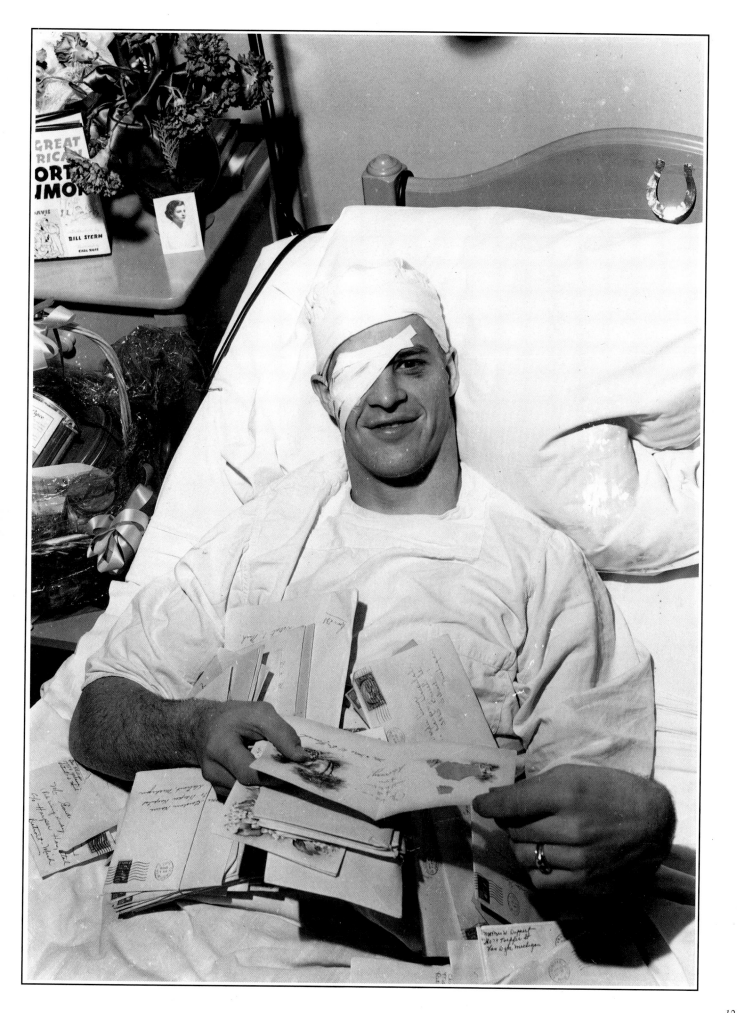

"Even Leswick was surprised. He just wanted to get rid of the thing."

- Butch Bouchard

Leswick's "fluke" stuns Canadiens

April 16, 1954

Goalie Terry Sawchuk kneels in front of the Stanley Cup as the Red Wings celebrate their victory. Coach Tommy Ivan (in suit and bow tie) is seen in the centre of the photo. Two players to the right of Ivan and facing the camera is Tony Leswick, who scored the winning goal in overtime.

Canadiens captain Butch Bouchard played on four Stanley Cup champions during his 15-year career. But his most vivid memory was the seventh-game overtime goal by Detroit's Tony Leswick that defeated Montreal in the 1954 finals. "To come so close to winning, then to lose on a fluke shot like Leswick's, that's still hard to take," Bouchard said years later.

The Montreal-Detroit rivalry had become the most intense in hockey. Partisans fiercely debated who was the more gifted goal scorer, Rocket Richard or Gordie Howe — or the superior defenceman, Doug Harvey or Red Kelly.

Just as they had the previous five seasons, the Red Wings concluded the regular season in top spot. In the semi-finals, Detroit overpowered Toronto in five games, while second-place Montreal, the defending Cup champions, needed just four games to dispense with the Boston Bruins.

Detroit entered the series as 2–1 favourites and made the odds-makers look good as they jumped out to a 3–1 lead after four games. For the fifth match Canadiens coach Dick Irvin switched goaltenders, replacing young Jacques Plante with veteran Gerry McNeil, who responded by shutting down the Wings as the Canadiens won 1–0 in overtime. Montreal took the next game 4–1 to set up a seventh-game showdown in Detroit.

The Wings, who had looked tired in game six, came out gunning, outshooting the Canadiens 33 to 23. But after Red Kelly scored to tie the game 1–1 in the second period, McNeil refused to be beaten.

Tony Leswick finally ended the drama with his "fluke" shot at 4:29 of extra play. As he headed to the Red Wing bench at the end of a shift, Leswick flipped the puck toward the Canadiens net. Doug Harvey reached up to knock it out of the air, but the puck ticked off his glove and over McNeil into the Montreal net.

"Even Leswick was surprised," remembered Butch Bouchard. "He had just wanted to get rid of the thing."

The stunned Canadiens stomped off the ice without stopping to congratulate their victorious rivals, an omission for which they were severely criticized.

"If I had shaken hands," answered Dick Irvin, "I wouldn't have meant it, and I refuse to be a hypocrite."

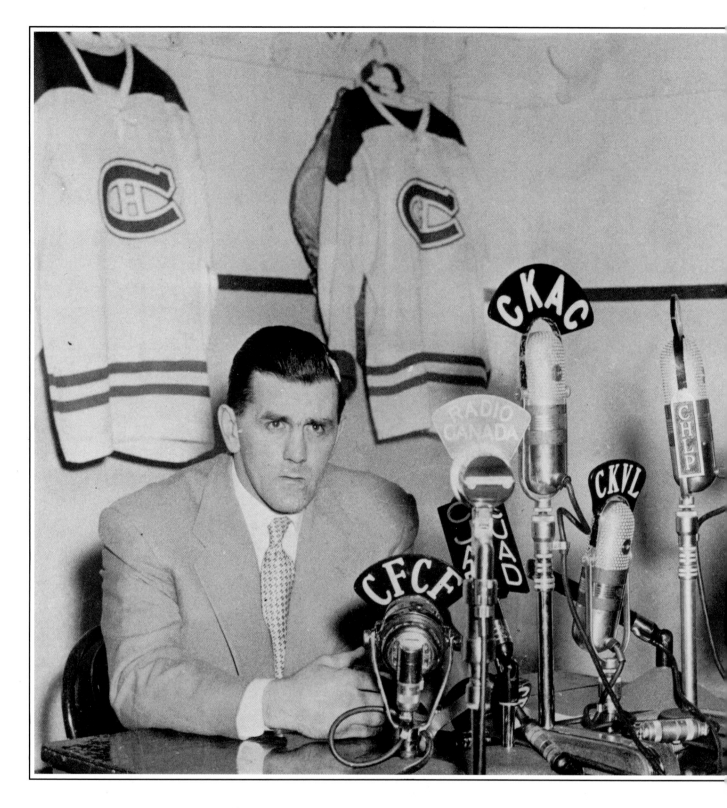

An eruption of the famous Richard temper cost him and the Canadiens dearly.

Montreal's night of darkness

March 17, 1955

Seated before a bank of microphones at a small table in the Canadiens dressing room, Richard, speaking in French and English, appealed to his fans for calm — "so that no further harm will be done. I will take my punishment and come back next year."

Coming down to the last week of the season, Maurice "Rocket" Richard was leading the league in points and had his heart set on winning his first scoring title. Montreal was also looking to end Detroit's run of six straight finishes atop the regular season standings.

Then, in Boston on March 13, an eruption of the famous Richard temper began a series of events that cost him and the Canadiens dearly. When Bruin Hal Laycoe cut Richard on top of the head, the Rocket first attacked Laycoe with his stick, and then turned on linesman Cliff Thompson with his fists when the official tried to intervene.

It was the second time that season that Richard had hit an official, and it was only one of many times that he had attacked an opponent with his stick. League president Clarence Campbell responded by suspending Richard for the final three games of the season and the entire playoffs.

Montreal fans were enraged. Many French Canadians even suggested that Campbell's decision was the result of an anti-French bias.

Campbell foolishly attended the next game at the Forum, when the Canadiens met the Wings in a showdown for first place. He was pelted with debris and then assaulted by a young man in a leather jacket. When a smoke bomb exploded, the building was ordered evacuated and Campbell declared the game forfeited to Detroit.

Once outside the arena, the fans went on a rampage that gained immediate infamy as the "Richard Riot." Windows were broken, stores looted, and more than 60 troublemakers arrested. The rioters caused an estimated $100,000 in damage.

The situation remained so volatile that the next evening Richard made a public appeal for calm. Although the crisis was defused, Quebec nationalists still regard the riot as a historic catalyst for the independence movement.

Richard finished one point behind teammate Bernie Geoffrion in the scoring race (he never came close again), Detroit took first place, and then the Red Wings barely edged the Rocketless Canadiens in a seven-game final.

Neither Richard nor the Montreal fans ever forgave Campbell for the suspension that cost them so much. "He was wrong," a still-bitter Rocket said when Campbell was buried in 1984.

Howe vs. Fontinato: fight night in New York

February 1, 1959

Most hockey fights are forgotten once the last punch is thrown. But the heavyweight bout between Gordie Howe and Lou Fontinato at New York's Madison Square Garden has lived on in memory. Howe rarely had to fight again, so fierce was the reputation he had earned from that one decision.

It happened in the first period of a game won by the Rangers 5–4. Fontinato felt Howe was picking on New York rookie Eddie Shack and decided to retaliate. Handy with his fists, Fontinato loved to fight. He made it his job to protect his teammates.

He challenged Howe behind the Detroit net. Howe accepted, and dropped his gloves. Then the two had at it for a full minute while their teammates and the officials watched in awe, unwilling to risk coming between the combatants.

"Howe began smashing him with lefts and rights, and then fired an uppercut that smashed Lou's nose," recounted referee Art Skov. "I just stood back and said, 'No way I'm going to break up this one.' Howe cleaned Fontinato like you've never seen." When the two finally separated, Fontinato's nose was smeared halfway across his face.

Years later the man known as "Leaping Lou" gave his own blow-by-blow description. "I gave Howe three of my best shots to the head and I peeked up to see why he hadn't gone down. Then pow! He hit me with this punch, just a short one, but it busted my nose all over the place, and broke blood vessels in my face — the whole bit."

Fontinato was taken to hospital, where he was photographed by *Life* magazine. Two weeks later a photo ran that showed him with blackened eyes staring out through bandages that almost completely covered his face.

"Howe needn't think he's Jack Dempsey just because he put me here," *Life* quoted a defiant Fontinato.

His adversary ignored the taunt. "I come to play hockey," Howe said, "not to fight." He seldom had to again.

> **"I just stood back and said, 'No way I'm going to break up this one.'"**
>
> *- Referee Art Skov*

Howe and Fontinato do battle behind the Detroit net in the photo above. Top right, a still defiant Fontinato is held back by teammate Eddie Shack and an official. Fontinato, his face grotesquely rearranged by a Howe uppercut, skates away in defeat in the final photo.

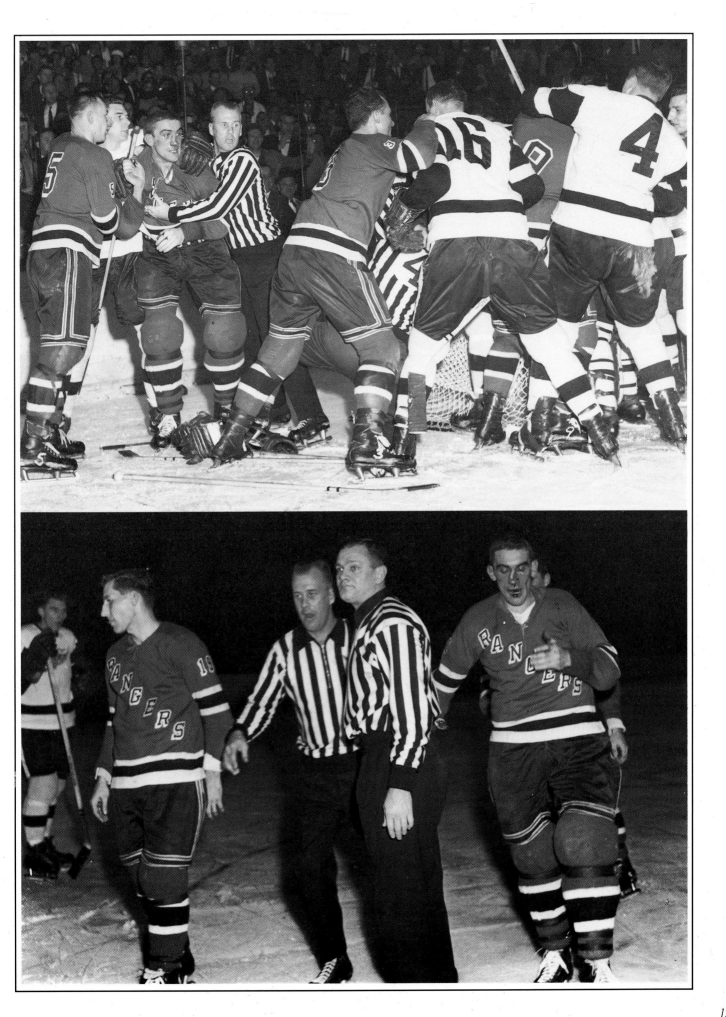

Last call for referee Red Storey

April 4, 1959

One spectator threw beer in Storey's face. Another jumped on him from behind.

He was willing to put up with the jeers of the crowd and even with spectators who climbed down from the stands and attacked him. But what combative and outspoken referee Red Storey refused to accept was public criticism from league president Clarence Campbell.

Storey was the head official for the sixth game of the semi-final between the Hawks and Canadiens in Chicago. Montreal led the series 3–2 and the game was tied 4–4 late in the third period when Chicago's Eddie Litzenberger fell to the ice after what the crowd thought was a trip by Montreal's Marcel Bonin. But Storey felt that Litzenberger had tripped himself. Montreal's Claude Provost picked up the loose puck and scored what proved to be the winning goal.

Seconds after play resumed, Bobby Hull was felled by Canadien Junior Langlois. "To the crowd it looked like a trip," recounted Storey, a former football star who once scored three touchdowns in a Grey Cup game for the Toronto Argonauts. "To me, there was no trip. Langlois hit Hull with a beautiful hip check."

That's when things turned ugly. The enraged crowd littered the ice with debris. One spectator hopped the boards and threw beer in Storey's face. Rushing to the ref's defence, Canadien Doug Harvey decked the intruder with a couple of punches. Another troublemaker jumped on Storey from behind. Harvey cut him with his stick for 18 stitches.

Play was interrupted for 25 minutes. After the game was finally played to its conclusion, Storey borrowed a stick and fought his way to the dressing room. Reflecting on his performance, Storey concluded that he'd "called a great game."

Clarence Campbell, who was in attendance, didn't agree, telling reporters that Storey "froze" and "choked up."

"I couldn't accept his comments and do my job, so I quit," said Storey, whose resignation was front-page news in NHL cities. He went on to a successful career in broadcasting and professed no lingering bitterness towards the fans who tried to kill him or the league president who undermined him.

"It was a privilege to referee in a decade, 1950 to 1960, that was the greatest in hockey history," Storey said. "I don't think hockey will ever reach that peak again."

"We're a couple of stubborn characters," Storey said of NHL president Clarence Campbell, who refused to retract his criticisms of the referee's performance in Chicago. "He had a league to run. I had my life to live. He was in a position where he couldn't back down. I was in a position that I couldn't accept it and do my job, so I resigned."

*The battle between
Geoffrion and
Mahovlich
culminated in
a showdown at
the Forum.*

Faceoff for 50

Checked closely by Habs defenceman Tom Johnson, Toronto's Frank Mahovlich breaks in on goalie Jacques Plante (top). Trailing the play is Mahovlich's rival in the race to score 50 goals, Bernie Geoffrion. After tying the record, Geoffrion receives congratulations from Rocket Richard.

March 16, 1961

For the first time since the spring of 1953, when Gordie Howe finished with 49 goals, there was a serious challenge to Rocket Richard's record of 50 goals in a season. The battle between Bernie "Boom Boom" Geoffrion of Montreal and Toronto's Frank Mahovlich to catch Richard culminated in a showdown at the Montreal Forum that had excited fans lining up around the block for standing-room tickets.

Chants of "Go! Go! Go! Bernie!" greeted local hero Geoffrion, who had 49 goals to 47 for Mahovlich, with two games remaining for both players after that night's match. The 30-year-old right winger had sizzled down the stretch, scoring 22 goals in his last 19 games. His sudden burst enabled him to pass Mahovlich, who had led the race most of the season but had gone cold in recent weeks.

Mahovlich, 23, managed just a single foiled shot on net as defensive specialist Claude Provost thwarted his every move. Geoffrion proved more difficult to contain. After narrowly missing on three previous scoring opportunities, he connected for his 50th goal at 14:15 of the third period.

Montreal was ahead 4–2 when linemate Jean Beliveau won a draw in the Leaf zone and passed to Gilles Tremblay at the right-wing boards. Tremblay fired a bullet pass across the goalmouth to a waiting Geoffrion. Before Toronto goaltender Cesare Maniago could react, the puck was in the open net.

A shower of programs and popcorn boxes rained down on the ice as Geoffrion did a little dance and then leaped into Beliveau's arms. His teammates jumped over the boards to join the celebration as attendants spent eight minutes cleaning up the debris.

"I'm glad it is over, that I have tied Rocket's record," Geoffrion managed between sobs and laughs after Montreal's 5–2 victory. "The pressure was terrible. Now I think I will break the record this weekend."

But Geoffrion was unable to score again, while Mahovlich added a single goal to his total before season's end. Boom Boom would have to be content with his second scoring title and a share of the record with his illustrious former teammate.

Beliveau wins the first Conn Smythe

May 1, 1965

Le Gros Bill, as Jean Beliveau was affectionately known to Montreal fans, had been the dominant performer throughout the 1965 playoffs.

"Even with our big teams [1955–60], he never had a series like it," said Canadiens coach Toe Blake in admiration. In the seven-game Cup final against the Chicago Black Hawks, Beliveau scored the winning goal three times and assisted on the other. His eight goals and eight assists in 13 playoff starts led the Canadiens to their 13th Stanley Cup title, and the first in five years.

As he had throughout the playoffs, Beliveau took charge from the opening whistle of the deciding game in Montreal. On learning that his line was going to start the game, he urged linemates Bobby Rousseau and Dick Duff to "have a good start so that the other lines would follow that way."

It took just 14 seconds for the tall captain to score what proved to be the winning goal. A pass from Duff hit Beliveau on the leg and bounced past goaltender Glenn Hall into the Chicago net.

"A bit lucky," admitted Beliveau afterwards. "I saw I couldn't get my stick to it, so I put my knees together and coasted into it. A perfect three-cushion billiard shot."

The Canadiens never let the Hawks back in the game. Less than five minutes later, Beliveau put a tremendous deke on Chicago defenceman Matt Ravlich before passing off to Duff, who whipped the puck past Hall on the right side. Montreal added two power play tallies in the same period and then coasted to a 4–0 victory.

In reward for his brilliance, Beliveau was named the inaugural winner of the Conn Smythe Trophy as the most valuable player in the playoffs. The trophy was donated by the Toronto Maple Leafs in honour of the team's former managing director.

"I had a feeling before the game that this was our night," said Beliveau. "I'm not saying I knew we'd have the winning goal after only 14 seconds, but I knew the puck was going into the Chicago zone right off the opening faceoff."

After big Jean's opening billiard shot, the Hawks had the sinking feeling that he was right.

> ## "Even with our big teams, he never had a series like it."
>
> *- Toe Blake*

Montreal captain Jean Beliveau smooches the brand-new Conn Smythe Trophy, which he won as the most valuable playoff performer. Donated by the Toronto Maple Leafs to honour the team's former managing director, the award included a $1,000 bonus.

Hull breaks the 50-goal barrier

March 12, 1966

Cavernous Chicago Stadium exploded with noise. Hats, umbrellas, newspapers, popcorn boxes, programs and souvenir pucks bearing the number 51 rained down on the ice. All 20,000 customers were on their feet, hugging, screaming, stomping and joyously pounding one another on the back.

Their darling, Bobby Hull, the blond Adonis who had become hockey's greatest star, had beaten New York's Cesare Maniago for his 51st goal at 5:34 of the third period, breaking the single-season mark he had shared with Montreal's Maurice Richard and Bernie "Boom Boom" Geoffrion.

Returning to the Chicago bench to escape the hail of debris, Hull was mobbed by his teammates. Then, grinning broadly and shaking the outstretched hands of the faithful, he skated along the boards to his wife Joanne's rinkside seat and clutched her hand over the Plexiglas barrier.

On his way back, Hull picked up a top hat from among the scattered litter and placed it jauntily on his head. Delighted, the crowd roared its devotion once again.

After the game, which the Hawks won 4–2, Hull described how he had taken a pass from teammate Lou Angotti just outside the Ranger blue line and skated in for the historic score.

"The Ranger defenders backed in and I moved ten feet over their blue line. I moved the puck out front for the slap shot.

"I got it out too far and almost topped it, didn't get real good wood on the thing and it skidded away, skimming the ice. I watched it all the way into the corner of the net."

Hull said he wasn't certain if the puck had deflected off teammate Eric Nesterenko.

"When the announcer said, 'Goal by Bobby Hull,' a great weight lifted off my shoulders. I can't describe the wonderful warm feeling I got when those fans let loose. I'll never forget that ovation. I have never heard anything like it and don't think I ever will again."

Hull went on to score 54 goals by season's end, and broke his own record in 1968–69 with 58.

The Golden Jet is pursued by Canadiens Dave Balon and Jacques Laperriere in the photo above. At right, Hull proudly displays the history-making puck.

"I'll never forget that ovation. I have never heard anything like it."

- Bobby Hull

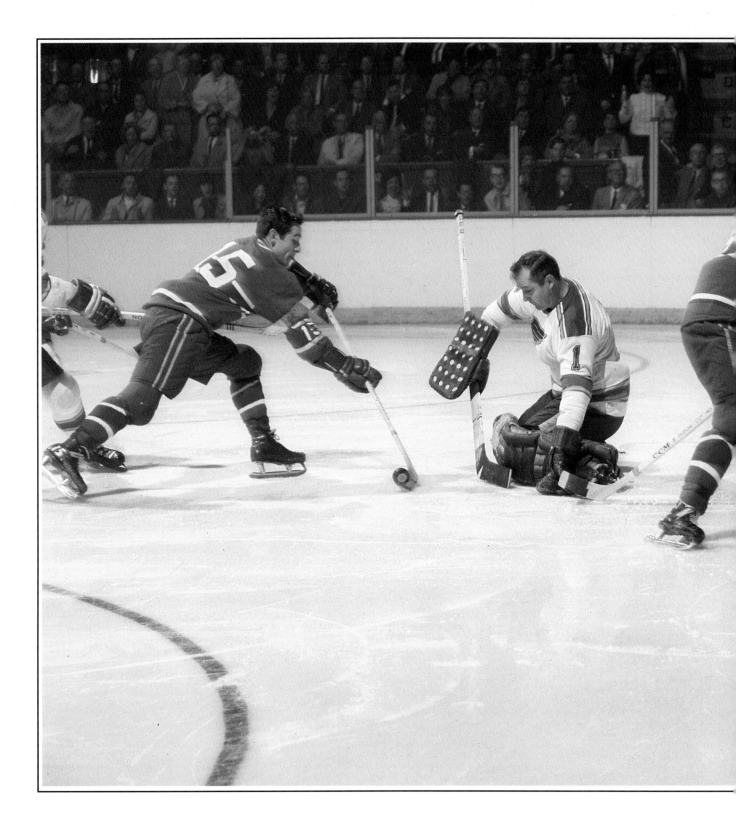

"It wasn't quite good enough, but it was good enough to scare the Canadiens."

- Glenn Hall

Glenn Hall gives Montreal the Blues

May 11, 1968

Montreal sniper Bobby Rousseau tests Glenn Hall, who was almost unbeatable throughout the playoffs. Although the Habs outshot the Blues 151–91, they outscored them by only four goals.

"There were times in that series when we were trying to get a puck past Hall that we asked each other, 'Will we ever beat this guy?'" remembered one Montreal player.

Future Hall-of-Famer Glenn Hall turned in four classic performances as the expansion St. Louis Blues lost 3–2, 1–0, 4–3 and 3–2 to the mighty Canadiens to bow out of the Stanley Cup final in consecutive games. All told, the Habs outshot St. Louis 151–91. In a total of 18 playoff games, Hall allowed only 45 scores.

Without him, the Cup final would have been no contest. The Blues were involved only because, as the winners of the all-expansion West Division, they were guaranteed a spot in the final. A two-time Vezina Trophy winner, Hall was one of the team's few frontline performers. The 36-year-old had reluctantly been made available in the expansion draft by his former employers, the Chicago Black Hawks, who felt obliged to protect younger talent.

Hall managed to keep the Blues in every game with his leaping, diving and altogether remarkable contortions in net. St. Louis lost all four matches by a single goal, and two of them went into overtime.

In the final game, played at the Montreal Forum, at least a dozen of the 27 shots fired at Hall required spectacular saves. The Canadiens finally got two goals past him in the third period for a 3–2 comeback victory.

"No one can be happy in defeat, but we have to feel good at extending the Canadiens in all four games," said Hall, who was named the winner of the Conn Smythe Trophy as the playoff's most valuable performer. It was the second time that a goalkeeper had been honoured since the award's inception in 1965. Like Roger Crozier, the Detroit backstop who won in 1966, Hall toiled for a team that had been bested by Montreal in the finals.

Hall looked around the dressing room at his teammates. "I don't rate all the credit," he said. "Every guy is bushed, worn out because he gave his best. It wasn't quite good enough, but it was good enough to scare the Canadiens."

Red Berenson's hat-trick times two

Few players have ever emerged so quickly from obscurity. Prior to the trade that sent him to the expansion St. Louis Blues from the New York Rangers the previous November, 28-year-old Red Berenson, who had broken in with Montreal in 1961, had never been more than a fringe player. Playing on a regular line at last, he immediately blossomed into one of the Blues top shooters, scoring 22 goals in 55 regular-season games and another five in the playoffs.

An amazing six-goal outburst in Philadelphia completed Berenson's transition into a star, and caused acute embarrassment for the general managers around the league who had failed to recognize the now obvious talents of the speedy red-haired centre.

Berenson scored his team's first five goals and added an assist and another score later on as the Blues trounced the Flyers 8–0. Four of the goals came in the second period, equalling the record for most goals in one frame held jointly by Harvey "Busher" Jackson and Max Bentley. His total of six goals tied the modern record set by Syd Howe of the Red Wings in 1944, and fell one short of Joe Malone's all-time record of seven, set in 1920.

"Tonight I had my confidence," said Berenson. "It's easy to skate when you get two goals early."

The six goals and one assist he tallied against the Flyers propelled him into second place in the scoring race, just two points behind Bobby Hull.

After the game, Berenson generously defended the play of Flyers goalie Doug Favell. "Three of the goals were breakaways, he was screened on two, and partially screened on another," he said. "It was difficult for him because he wasn't getting a lot of shots except when I came down."

Berenson also pointed out that he'd hit a post and missed on two other excellent chances. A benchwarmer less than a year before, hockey's newest star felt cheated that he hadn't scored two or three more.

Hockey's newest star felt cheated that he hadn't scored two or three more.

Used as a spare forward and penalty killer until he was acquired by St. Louis, Berenson scored 35 goals in 1968–69 and 261 in 17 NHL seasons.

Orr wins a scoring title but wants more

For someone who had so many personal achievements to celebrate, Bobby Orr was in a decidedly dark mood as the regular season came to a close.

Orr and the rest of the Boston Bruins were in their dressing room after a victory over Toronto that they hoped would secure them a first-place finish ahead of Chicago. Then they heard on the radio that the Hawks were romping to a triumph over the Canadiens. Although both teams would finish with 99 points, Chicago took the title on the strength of more wins.

"Get those radios out of here," barked Orr, who had become the first defenceman in history to win a scoring title. "I don't want to hear the bad news."

The 22-year-old was a man on a mission. Orr wouldn't rest until he had helped bring home Boston's first Stanley Cup since 1941.

He had maintained a torrid scoring pace right from the start of the season. His total of 87 assists topped the record of 77 set the season before by teammate Phil Esposito, and his 33 goals shattered his own record of 21 for a defencemen, which he had established the year before. Orr's final tally of 120 points came within six of Esposito's all-time mark.

Many longtime fans were calling him the greatest player who ever lived. But for the moment, the young star couldn't see beyond his team's disappointing second-place finish.

A photographer thoughtlessly asked Orr to pose with one of the champagne bottles that had been on hand to help celebrate a league championship. "Get lost," he snarled. "I don't even like the stuff."

A little over a month later teammates would shower him in bubbly after he scored the winning goal in Boston's Stanley Cup triumph over St. Louis. Awarded the Conn Smythe Trophy as the most valuable performer in the playoffs, Orr thus became the first player in history to win four individual trophies in the same season: the Norris for top defenceman, the Hart as most valuable player, the Art Ross as top scorer, and the Conn Smythe.

Mission more than accomplished.

Orr wouldn't rest until he had helped bring home Boston's first Stanley Cup since 1941.

No defenceman — and few other players — have ever dominated the game in the manner of Bobby Orr. "Bobby was a star from the moment they played the national anthem in his first NHL game," said Boston coach Harry Sinden. Orr's first scoring championship in 1969–70 was followed by a second in 1974–75, when he scored a career-high 46 goals.

The brothers Dryden make goaltending history

March 20, 1971

> *"Seeing Dave in the other goal was a distraction I didn't want or need."*
>
> *- Ken Dryden*

Dave Dryden (near left) told reporters that he had always hoped to get a chance to play against his kid brother in the NHL. "I was family-proud that my brother was at the other end of the rink," he said. "There are six years' difference in our ages and I was always coaching him when we were kids. It looks like he's going to be a good one."

Despite the best efforts of Buffalo coach and master showman Punch Imlach, the first confrontation between goaltending brothers in NHL history almost didn't happen.

Imlach had hoped to stir up a little excitement for the otherwise meaningless late-season game at the Montreal Forum by starting veteran Dave Dryden in goal for the Sabres. He assumed that Montreal coach Al MacNeil would play along by putting Dryden's younger brother Ken, a recent call-up from the minors, in goal for the Canadiens. But MacNeil opted to go with Rogie Vachon instead.

"I thought starting the brothers right off the bat would be a helluva deal for the crowd," said Imlach. "But MacNeil didn't want to give the fans a run for their money until he had to."

Imlach couldn't understand why MacNeil chose to play the spoilsport. The Sabres, then in their first year of operation, were out of the playoff hunt; the Canadiens already had a lock on their spot in post-season play. Disgruntled, Imlach switched to his alternate netminder Joe Daley two minutes before faceoff.

Then luck — or, rather, the bad luck of Rogie Vachon — intervened. With the Canadiens leading 2–0 in the second period, Vachon was injured and had to be removed from the game. Out skated 23-year-old Ken Dryden. Imlach immediately put in brother Dave, 29, a five-year veteran of the NHL wars.

Both brothers admitted they had the jitters as play resumed at 13:07. Dave looked terrible on the first shot he faced, missing Jacques Lemaire's 85-footer. Then he pulled himself together and made 17 stops before the final buzzer. Ken handled 15 chances, allowing two goals in the third period as the Sabres briefly rallied. The final score was 5–2 for Montreal.

As the crowd cheered warmly, the brothers met at centre ice and shook hands.

Years later in his autobiography, *The Game*, Ken Dryden recalled the night he and his big brother made history. "I didn't enjoy that game very much," he wrote. "I had played only two previous NHL games, and seeing Dave in the other goal was a distraction I didn't want or need."

Espo's speech rallies Team Canada

September 8, 1972

Team Canada was *supposed* to be the greatest collection of hockey players ever assembled on one team, and yet they had broken the hearts of fans across the country by losing the Canadian portion of the eight-game summit series with the Soviet Union. Never mind that the Soviets were the defending Olympic champions and had won nine IIHF World Amateur Championships since 1963. Hockey, Canadians had always believed, was their game.

That night in Vancouver many of the 18,000 in attendance had actually taunted and booed the members of Team Canada, who looked miserable in a 5–3 defeat that put their record in the series at one win, a tie and two losses. Afterwards, one of the few Canadians who had played well decided to speak out.

"To the people across Canada, we're trying our best," a sweating, emotionally drawn Phil Esposito told a national television audience immediately after the game. "We're all disappointed, disenchanted. I can't believe people are booing us. If the Russians boo their players like some of our Canadian fans — not all, just some — then I'll come back and apologize.

"We're completely disappointed. I can't believe it. We're trying hard. They've got a good team. We're all here because we love Canada. It's our home and that's the only reason we came."

The other players unanimously supported the sentiments expressed by Esposito, who from that moment became the team's spiritual and physical leader. Added goaltender Ken Dryden, "What happened was this: We were going to have a big party and the Russians spoiled it."

Many Canadians felt shamed by Esposito's oratory. Team Canada received hundreds of telegrams saying that, win or lose, the criticism would stop. Few now expected the Canadians to win more than a game in Moscow. One newspaper reporter likened their upcoming journey to an earlier one taken by Napoleon, and predicted similarly disastrous results.

But, thanks to the leadership of Phil Esposito and three timely goals by a left winger named Paul Henderson, it would be the Russians who met their Waterloo.

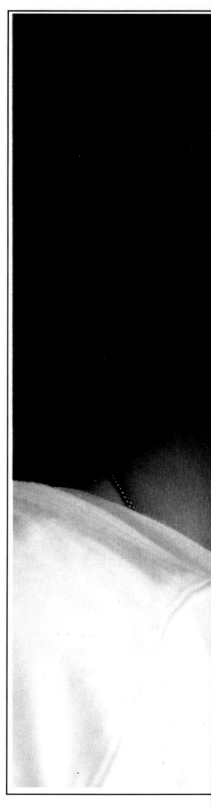

Esposito's emotional outburst came during a television interview following Team Canada's 5–3 loss in Vancouver. Many observers felt that for the eight games of the summit series, Esposito was the greatest — and certainly most inspirational — hockey player who ever lived.

"We're all disappointed.
I can't believe people
are booing us."

- Phil Esposito

*"I hope this has
convinced people
we can play
hockey."*

- Bobby Clarke

Flyers first expansion champs

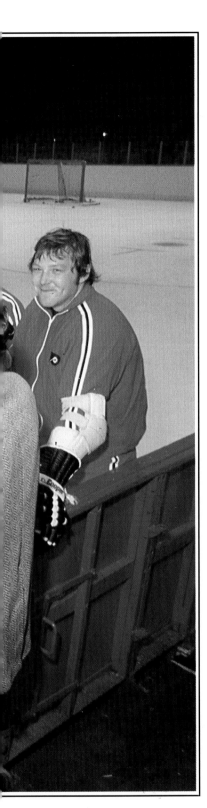

Coach Fred Shero's Philadelphia Flyers not only became the first expansion team to win a game in the finals, but beat Bobby Orr and the Big Bad Bruins in six to capture the Cup.

They were known derisively as the "Animals" and the "Broad Street Bullies." During the regular season the Philadelphia Flyers spent more time in the penalty box than any other team in history.

But with captain Bobby Clarke and snipers Bill Barber and Rick MacLeish leading the attack, and Vezina Trophy winner Bernie Parent in net, the Flyers were a more highly skilled squad than their critics gave them credit for.

Still, they weren't given much of a chance as they faced off against the high-scoring Boston Bruins in the Stanley Cup finals. It was tough to bet against a team whose lineup included both Bobby Orr and Phil Esposito.

To that point, no expansion team had won even a single game in the finals. Orr made certain the losing streak continued when he split through the Flyer defence and beat Parent to break a 2–2 deadlock with less than 30 seconds remaining in the third period of the first game.

Two nights later, Clarke, who consistently outplayed rival centre Esposito, ended the expansion hex with an overtime goal that won the game 3–2. The Flyers also took the third game in Philadelphia 4–1, and the next one 4–2 to close within one game of becoming the first expansion club to win a Stanley Cup.

Bobby Orr scored two goals in the fifth game to almost single-handedly stave off elimination as the Bruins won 5–1. But even hockey's greatest star couldn't stop the Flyers back in Philadelphia.

Bernie Parent was magnificent once again, turning back drive after drive, most of them orchestrated by Orr. The Flyers scored the game's only goal, the Cup winner, at 14:48 of the first period, when Moose Dupont's shot from the point deflected off Rick MacLeish into the Bruin net. Then Parent, who would win the Conn Smythe Trophy as the most valuable player in the playoffs, closed the door.

"We've taken a lot of bum raps all season about being bullies," said a jubilant Bobby Clarke. "I hope this has convinced people we can play hockey and are worthy Stanley Cup champions."

Toronto's Ian Turnbull gets "lucky"

Although considered one of the most gifted scorers among NHL defencemen, Toronto's Ian Turnbull had only recently ended a frustrating 30-game goalless drought. He still didn't feel that he had regained his touch around the net. Then Turnbull scored five goals in one incredible night to set an all-time record for defencemen.

"I guess I just got lucky," said the 23-year-old, whose five goals came on only five shots as the Maple Leafs clobbered the Red Wings 9–1 in Toronto. "A couple [of the goals] were easy and a couple of others were lucky. It was one of those nights when everything goes in."

His first goal, one of the lucky ones, came at 1:55 of the second period. Turnbull let go a low shot from the point that deflected off Red Wing defenceman Terry Harper into the net past goaltender Ed Giacomin.

The second goal, at 10:26 of the same frame, was prettier. With each team playing two men short, Turnbull intercepted a pass in the Detroit zone and blasted the puck past a helpless Giacomin.

Detroit replaced Giacomin with Jim Rutherford at the start of the third period, but by this point the Leafs and Turnbull were unstoppable.

Leading a charge up the left side, Turnbull unleashed a slapshot that almost tore off Rutherford's glove. That goal, at 2:32, gave him his first NHL hat-trick.

Luck intervened again on his next one, at 17:10, which tied him with five other defencemen who had scored four goals in one game. Cruising in front of the net, Turnbull was upended by Rutherford; a shot by teammate Stan Weir bounced off his arm into the net.

With less than three minutes remaining to play, Turnbull and his mates decided to go full-out for the record. "The whole idea was to head-man the puck, and everything went just as planned," Turnbull recounted.

A minute and 20 seconds after his fourth goal, Turnbull was fed a perfect pass by his defence partner, Borje Salming, and fired a low shot past Rutherford.

Hockey's newest record holder could offer no explanation for his suddenly hot hand — except the obvious one. "You just get lucky every now and again," Turnbull shrugged.

"It was one of those nights when everything goes in."

- Ian Turnbull

An obviously thrilled Ian Turnbull puts his record fifth goal of the game past Detroit's Jim Rutherford (top right). A little over a month later at Maple Leaf Gardens, NHL president Clarence Campbell commemorated the event by presenting a silver tea set to Turnbull and his wife Inga.

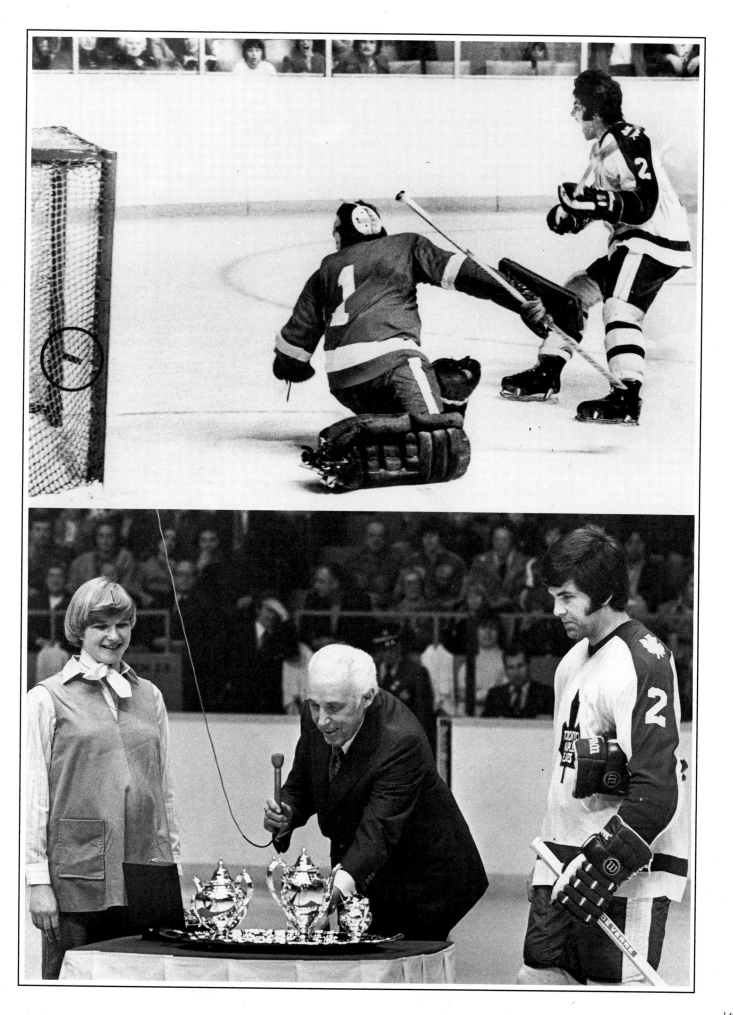

A fast 50 and then Gretzky catches Espo

February 24, 1982

Not Richard, Howe, Hull or any other of the game's greatest names has ever dominated a season so completely as Wayne Gretzky did in 1981–82.

Still weeks shy of his 21st birthday, the Edmonton Oiler sensation scored five times against the Philadelphia Flyers on December 30 to raise his season's total to an incredible 50 in his first 39 games — 11 fewer matches than were required by Mike Bossy the previous season and Maurice Richard back in 1944–45 to achieve the 50-in-50 milestone.

Gretzky's 50th was an empty net goal that sealed a 7–5 Oilers triumph with just three seconds left in the third period. As the sellout crowd at Edmonton's Northlands Coliseum offered a deafening tribute, Gretzky was mobbed by his teammates.

"I really didn't say anything about 50 in 50, but there was a lot of pressure put on me by other people and I felt it," No. 99 said afterwards.

He was asked to compare his accomplishment to that of Maurice Richard, who played in the more defence-oriented six-team era. "What Maurice Richard did wasn't broken tonight," Gretzky answered diplomatically. "It will still stand. The league was really strong then. Hockey is a lot different game now."

After having scored 50 goals so quickly, there was little doubt that Gretzky would go on to obliterate Phil Esposito's single-season, goal-scoring record of 76 in 78 games, set in 1970–71. On February 24, in just his 64th game, Gretzky fired his 77th goal past Buffalo goaltender Don Edwards. He finished the campaign with 92 goals and also improved by 44 the points record of 164 he had set the season before.

Many who watched him that season were convinced Gretzky was establishing records so remarkable that they might never again be approached, not even by himself. But the wunderkind already known as "the Great One" believed that all records were made to be broken.

"This record will probably fall," he had said after scoring his 50th in the 39th game. "I don't know in how many years. I just know it will fall."

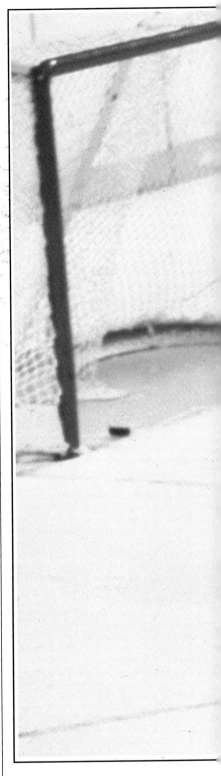

Wayne Gretzky beats Buffalo goalie Don Edwards for his 77th goal of the season to eclipse Phil Esposito's old single-season mark. Gretzky's record breaker came in just his 64th game.

Many were convinced that Gretzky was establishing records that might never again be approached.

Another American first for Bobby Carpenter

March 21, 1985

"It's special to score the 50th goal, you've got to feel honoured."

- Bobby Carpenter

By this point, breaking new ground had become almost routine for the Washington Capitals U.S.-born phenom Bobby Carpenter. He was already the first of his countrymen to be drafted in the first round of an NHL entry draft (third overall in 1981), and then he'd been the first to make the leap directly from high school hockey to the big time.

Just 21 and in his fourth season with the Capitals, the "Can't Miss Kid," as Carpenter had been labelled when he was starring at St. John's Prep School in Massachusetts, was an inspiration for young hockey players throughout the United States.

Several games back he'd passed the previous American-high mark of 41 goals, set the season before by Joe Mullen of the St. Louis Blues. Now, at the Montreal Forum, he joined Jari Kurri, a native of Finland, and Ken Hodge, who was born in England, as just the third non-Canadian native to score 50 times in a season.

The goal came on a power play at 15:24 of the second period. Carpenter, who had set up Mike Gartner for the Capitals other score in a 3–2 losing effort, snared a rebound in front of the net and snapped a wrist shot past Canadiens goaltender Steve Penney.

"It's special to score the 50th goal, you've got to feel honoured," said Carpenter, who added three more goals to his total before the season ended.

He felt he had been pressing in recent games as the prize drew nearer. "There's no way you play your normal game, because it's always there in the back of your mind. It seems that when you try not to think about it, that's when you think about it the most."

Carpenter expressed the hope that his accomplishments would encourage NHL scouts to recruit more American players.

Washington coach Bryan Murray felt certain it would, and added, "This is a remarkable achievement for a guy who has come out of high school and really had to grow up in the best league in the world."

Carpenter was rewarded for his 53-goal season with a four-year contract said to be worth $1.3 million — another record for an American-born player.

Goalie Ron Hextall shoots and scores

December 8, 1987

"I knew it was just a matter of time before I flipped one in."

- Ron Hextall

Ranger goalie Chuck Raynor had given it a heck of a try during a game in 1947, making three mad dashes into the Montreal zone to try to score the tying goal in a 2–1 New York loss. Billy Smith of the New York Islanders had been credited with one on November 28, 1979, although that was only because he was the last Islander to touch the puck before a Colorado defenceman put it in his own net.

Until Ron Hextall managed the feat in Philadelphia against the Boston Bruins, no netminder had actually shot the puck into an opponent's net for a goal. "I don't mean to sound cocky," said Hextall afterwards, "but I knew it was just a matter of time before I flipped one in."

An aggressive puck handler who often strayed far out of his net to stop long shots at the boards and direct passes to his defencemen, Hextall scored his goal late in the third period with the Flyers ahead 4–2. Boston goalie Rejean Lemelin had been called to the bench in favour of an extra attacker.

Hextall got hold of a loose puck, took aim and flipped a high shot into the air toward the Boston net. The puck landed near the Boston blue line and then bounced into the empty cage.

"I looked up and saw the open ice," recounted an excited Hextall, who the season before had won the Vezina Trophy in his rookie campaign. "I was hoping to get the puck close. I shot it and saw it roll in."

Hextall's was the final tally in a 5–2 Philadelphia victory. League statisticians announced that it had taken 40,219 NHL games for a goalie to shoot a puck for a goal.

The next one wouldn't take nearly as long. In a playoff match against Washington the following season, Hextall shot the puck the length of the ice into an empty net for his second career score, and the first by a goalie in Stanley Cup play.

"Bobby Orr, Wayne Gretzky, Mario Lemieux, they all changed the game," said an admiring David Poile, the Washington general manager. "Now Hextall's changing it too."

"It was a perfect opportunity for me with us being up two goals at the time," said Hextall of his decision to shoot to score. No goalie in 40,218 previous NHL games had ever managed the feat.

155

Marvellous Mario shoots for the cycle

December 31, 1988

> *Lemieux's accomplishment was hailed as the most secure record in the book.*

Even teammates who watched his nightly magic act were awed by Mario Lemieux's groundbreaking performance against the New Jersey Devils on New Year's Eve. "He put the puck through his legs, he made some twirls; the things he did out there were amazing," said Lemieux's linemate Rob Brown.

In registering his first five-goal game in the NHL, the 23-year-old — known variously as "Marvellous Mario" and "Mario the Magnificent" — became the only player in history to score in every conceivable fashion: at even strength, on a power play, while the Penguins were shorthanded, on a penalty shot and, finally, into an empty net.

It was like hitting for the cycle in baseball — only this was perhaps a thousand times more improbable, largely because penalty shots are so rarely called (Lemieux had two previous penalty shots in his five-year career, and had scored each time). His accomplishment was immediately hailed as the most secure record in the book.

Lemieux's five goals and three assists in the Penguins 8–6 home-ice defeat of New Jersey set a Pittsburgh team record for goals in a game, and tied his own team mark for points in a single match, which he had accomplished earlier in the season against St. Louis. Wayne Gretzky was the only other player to record two eight-point games in the same season.

Racing toward his second consecutive scoring championship, Lemieux now had 104 points to lead the league. His climb to the 100-point level was the third-fastest in NHL history, trailing only Gretzky's performances in 1983–84 and 1984–85.

A reporter had the temerity to mention Gretzky's name in the Pittsburgh dressing room, but Rob Brown would brook no comparisons. Lemieux was, Brown insisted, "the best hockey player in the world."

The hero himself theorized that he had played so well because he had been excused from practice the previous day.

"The day off helped me a lot," Marvellous Mario said. "I felt pretty good."

Pittsburgh's Mario Lemieux scored at even strength, on a power play, while his team was shorthanded, on a penalty shot and into an empty net to become the first player in NHL history to shoot for the cycle.

"It has been said that I stuck with the old men
so long we couldn't possibly win the
Stanley Cup. For some of you it's a farewell.
Go out there and put that puck down their throats!"

- Toronto coach Punch Imlach
before the final game of the 1967 playoffs

Debuts, galas and farewells

Montreal wins first Cup showdown

March 22, 1894

"The referee forgot to see many things."

- Montreal Gazette

"I have for some time been thinking that it would be a good thing if there were a challenge cup which should be held from year to year by the champion hockey team in the Dominion of Canada."

In the more than 100 years since Lord Stanley of Preston, then Canada's governor general, made his announcement, the battered old trophy that bears his name has become one of the most famous icons in all of sport. Almost from its inception, hockey's greatest players considered their careers incomplete until they had sipped champagne from the silver bowl, which had cost his lordship $48.67.

The first presentation of the Stanley Cup was made in 1893 to the Montreal Amateur Athletic Association, champions of the Amateur Hockey Association, then considered the best league in the country. As league champions, Montreal AAA received automatic possession of the new award, but were required to accept any challenges. When none appeared, Montreal's possession remained uncontested until the end of the next season.

On March 22, 1894, the first Stanley Cup match was played between the defending champion Montreal AAA (now renamed the Montreal Hockey Club) and the Ottawa Capitals.

By all reports, excitement ran high for the one-game, winner-take-all confrontation in Montreal. An estimated 5,000 fans were in attendance, having paid 25 cents for rush seats and 75 cents and a dollar for reserved seating.

Montreal won 3–1, with little Billy Barlow emerging as the first Stanley Cup hero. Barlow put two shots, including the winner, through the upright poles that served as goals in those early days. The game account in the Montreal *Gazette* included the wry observation that "the referee forgot to see many things."

Unfortunately, Lord Stanley wasn't in Montreal for the game. When his older brother died early in 1893, he had returned permanently to England to attend to family affairs. Left behind was the silver bowl that became the game's most important legacy.

It is said that Lord Stanley (left) was persuaded by his sons Arthur and Algy, who had become enthusiastic adherents of the game, to donate the silver bowl that became known as the Stanley Cup. His lordship was back home in England by the time Montreal AAA (above) defeated the Ottawa Capitals in the first title game.

The Cup goes West

Founded just over three years before by hockey pioneers Frank and Lester Patrick, the Pacific Coast Hockey Association had by 1914–15 grown to rival the National Hockey Association (the predecessor of the NHL) in its ability to attract the best players of the day. Among the luminaries who had gone west to ply their trade was the era's greatest star, Fred "Cyclone" Taylor, who led Frank Patrick's Vancouver Millionaires to the PCHA championship.

There was general agreement that the game could only profit from an East-West rivalry. So that March the Ottawa Senators, as champions of the NHA, were sent west to engage Vancouver in what was expected to become an annual event. Never before had a Cup series been played west of Winnipeg.

Both squads were loaded with talent. The Ottawa attack was led by Jack Darragh, Punch Broadbent and Eddie Gerard; Vancouver's lineup included Mickey MacKay, Barney Stanley, Frank Nighbor and, of course, the incomparable Cyclone Taylor, who had once skated for Ottawa. All of the aforementioned were eventually voted into the Hockey Hall of Fame.

Vancouver was in a fever of excitement when the best-of-five series began, and the pitch intensified as the Millionaires quickly proved their superiority. Taylor scored twice in the opener as Vancouver won 6–2, and he and Nighbor both had hat-tricks when the Millionaires breezed to an 8–3 victory in the second match.

"Cyclone Taylor was the best hockey player in the world when he left Ottawa, and if possible he is even better now," said Senators manager Frank Shaughnessy. "He is amazing."

In the third and deciding contest, Ottawa managed to hold Taylor off the scoresheet, but the rest of the Millionaires were left free to attack almost at will, running up the score to 12–3. As the victors, the Millionaires each received a $300 share of the series money.

Years later those who saw them demolish Ottawa remembered the Millionaires with awe. Said Lester Patrick, the game's legendary Silver Fox who was then running the PCHA's Victoria entry: "That Vancouver team my brother assembled in 1914–15 was the greatest team I ever saw."

*Frank Patrick (left) and his brother
Lester brought big-time hockey to the
West Coast when they founded the
PCHA. Following a last-place finish in
1913–14, the Millionaires rebounded
to win their league title and challenge
for the Stanley Cup. The legendary
Fred "Cyclone" Taylor (second from the
left in the back row of the team photo)
scored five goals for Vancouver in the
three-game final.*

"*That Vancouver
team my brother
assembled was the
greatest team I
ever saw.*"

- Lester Patrick

Foster Hewitt's first radio broadcast

March 22, 1923

"He shoots! He scores!" shouted Hewitt for the first time.

"Hello, Canada, and hockey fans in the United States and Newfoundland..."

Every Saturday night from Toronto's Maple Leaf Gardens, broadcasting pioneer Foster Hewitt greeted his millions of listeners with these familiar words. By the 1930s he had become the most famous man in Canada, receiving as many as 90,000 letters a year from his fans. Today those early broadcasts are credited with having helped unify a vast, sparsely populated land.

Just 20 when he broadcast his first hockey match on March 22, 1923, Hewitt was an employee of *The Toronto Star.* The newspaper was setting up Ontario's first radio station, CFCA. It was only the second time a hockey game had been aired over radio.

Hewitt's assignment was an intermediate-level match at the Mutual Street Arena. He broadcast via a telephone hook-up from a tiny, glass-enclosed booth.

"I started to suffocate because it had no air holes," Hewitt later recalled. The glass kept fogging up, and he had to continually wipe it to get even a hazy view of the players.

Sometime that night, in his slightly falsetto voice, Hewitt first yelled the excited phrase that was to become his trademark: "He shoots! He scores!"

Drenched in sweat, an exhausted Hewitt finished the game and vowed that it would be his last. But the next day dozens of enthusiastic letters arrived at the *Star* and he was pressured to continue.

By the time Maple Leaf Gardens opened in 1931, Hewitt had exclusive rights to broadcast Maple Leaf games. He worked from the gondola, a perch 56 feet above ice level that had been given its name by a visitor who said "it looks just like the gondola on an airship."

By 1933, hockey's most famous voice was being heard on 20 stations across the country. Hewitt went on to broadcast the first televised hockey game in Canada on November 1, 1952, and he continued to work on both radio and television until 1978.

Hewitt's fame never dimmed. Speaking for several generations of fans, Bobby Hull once said, "When I met him, it was like meeting God."

Hewitt hadn't enjoyed the experience of broadcasting his first game. "If I had been permitted first choice," he said later, "that would have been my first, last and only broadcast."

A housewarming present for Toronto

April 9, 1932

It was certainly a season Toronto Maple Leaf fans would long remember. On November 12, 1931, the team had taken up residence in Maple Leaf Gardens, a sparkling new $1.5 million ice palace that (thanks to the radio broadcasts of Foster Hewitt) would soon become something close to a shrine for fans across the country. Torontonians had watched in awe as the building was completed in just five months.

Many in the opening night crowd of 13,542 were dressed in formal evening wear. During the pre-game ceremony the bands of the 48th Highlanders and the Toronto Irish Regiment joined in a rousing rendition of "Happy Days Are Here Again," a portentous selection in that the Leafs were about to embark on an extended run of excellence. Only the Montreal Canadiens would win more Stanley Cups in the years ahead.

Capacity audiences filled the arena the rest of the season to cheer a home team that featured the league's most potent offence. Leading the attack was the famous Kid Line of Harvey "Busher" Jackson, Joe Primeau and Charlie Conacher, who finished first, second and fourth in the scoring race.

After placing second behind the Canadiens during the regular season, the Leafs eliminated Chicago and then the Montreal Maroons. In the finals, Toronto overwhelmed the New York Rangers in three straight to capture the city's first Cup since the Leafs forebears, the St. Pats, had turned the trick in 1922. No team before them had ever taken a best-of-five final series in the minimum three games.

The victory was won on home ice, and afterwards hundreds of Toronto fans lingered long after the on-ice celebrations were over, jamming the runways leading to the Leafs dressing room. Local daily *The Globe* reported that "they appeared reluctant to leave this scene of one of Toronto's greatest hockey triumphs, until they had personally congratulated the men responsible for it."

The Maple Leafs overwhelmed the Rangers in three straight to capture the city's first Cup since 1922.

The famous Kid Line of Charlie Conacher, Joe Primeau and Harvey "Busher" Jackson (pictured at right) combined for 75 goals to lead the league's most potent attack. Left winger Jackson topped all scorers with 53 points, and Primeau was awarded the Lady Byng Trophy as the player best combining sportsmanship and gentlemanly conduct with a high standard of play.

King Clancy's coronation

March 17, 1934

In the years following his purchase from Ottawa in 1930, King Clancy captured the hearts of Toronto fans like few players have before or since. They thrilled to his head-long rushes into the enemy zone, and admired him for having a heart too big ever to admit defeat. It was obvious to everyone just how much the irrepressible little Irishman loved to play the game.

So it was with a good measure of enthusiasm that a crowd of 11,000 turned out for King Clancy Night on St. Patrick's Day in 1934. Maple Leaf Gardens was decorated for the occasion in green and orange bunting, and the Knights of Columbus Minstrel Band played Irish airs.

Before the start of the game with the New York Rangers, a procession of floats delighted the crowd. Several junior players stepped out of a large potato, then the combative Red Horner emerged from a boxing glove. Ranger star Bill Cook hid in a shamrock.

Finally, after the lights had been dimmed, Clancy, seated on a float in the shape of a throne, was pushed to centre ice. He was made up like Old King Cole, complete with beard, a silver crown and flowing robes.

After being helped down by his teammates, who playfully smeared coal dust over his face, Clancy removed his robe to reveal that he was wearing a green uniform decorated with a large shamrock on the back.

He accepted a grandfather clock as well as other gifts, thanked the crowd, then skated out to start the game, still dressed in green. At the end of the first period when Ranger coach Lester Patrick complained that his players found the green shirt too distracting, Clancy changed back into his Toronto blues.

The Leafs went on to win the game 3–2, an outcome Toronto fans were quick to credit to the luck of the Irish.

The popular star's big night was almost half an hour late in starting to accommodate hundreds of fans who lined up outside in the rain for tickets.

He was made up
like Old King
Cole, complete
with a crown and
flowing robes.

They called him Mr. Zero

December 1, 1938

When the Bruins sold four-time Vezina Trophy winning goaltender Tiny Thompson to Detroit at the end of November, 1938, local papers said that Boston fans hadn't had such a shock since Babe Ruth had been sent packing to the New York Yankees. It was difficult for anyone to imagine how Thompson's replacement, 23-year-old Frankie Brimsek, just arrived from the farm team in Providence, could fill such big shoes.

But Bruin boss Art Ross felt certain he'd made the right decision. Brimsek's quickness with his glove hand had convinced Ross to give him the job. "His hands are like lightning — the quickest I ever saw," he told reporters.

Brimsek immediately justified Ross's faith. He was brilliant in his first game December 1, even though the Bruins lost to Montreal 2–0. His next time out, on December 4 in Chicago, he shut down the Hawks 5–0. In his Boston debut two nights later, he blanked Chicago 2–0. Then he stonewalled the Rangers 3–0.

Until the Rangers got to him for two goals in his next outing, another Bruin victory, he had 231 minutes, 54 seconds of scoreless play to his credit. Then he shut out Montreal, Detroit and the New York Americans for a scoreless run of 220 minutes, 24 seconds.

By now Brimsek was the talk of hockey and had been given the nickname that would stick with him for the remainder of his career — Mr. Zero. Another handle the writers pinned on him was Frigid Frank, because he was supposedly so cool in a crisis.

That year Brimsek was named the league's top rookie, earned a spot on the first all-star team, and won the Vezina Trophy on the strength of his 1.59 goals-against average. Boston won the Stanley Cup by defeating Toronto in five games as Brimsek surrendered just six goals.

No goalie in history has ever made such a spectacular debut. But Brimsek refused to take it all too seriously. "Goaltending," he was fond of saying, "is mostly luck."

Contributing to the tremendous popularity Brimsek would come to enjoy in Boston was the fact that he was an American, born and raised in Eveleth, Minnesota. Brimsek backstopped the Bruins to two Stanley Cups in his first three seasons.

"His hands are like lightning — the quickest I ever saw."

- Art Ross

A last sip for the Broadway Blueshirts

April 13, 1940

For New York fans, the brief, long-ago era of Ranger brilliance now seems almost like the Camelot of Arthurian legend; a dimly remembered, happier time when the Rangers thrice held aloft hockey's Holy Grail, the Stanley Cup.

Coached by Lester Patrick, the legendary Silver Fox, the Rangers had won the Cup in 1928 and 1933 and continued to be one of the game's premier attractions, heralded in newspaper advertisements as "The Broadway Blueshirts...Classiest Team in Hockey." Adding to their aura were such high-profile Ranger-boosters as George Raft, Humphrey Bogart and Babe Ruth.

Now coached by Frank Boucher with Patrick attending to administrative duties, the 1940 Rangers were a fast-skating squad that specialized in precise passing in the enemy zone. The offence was led by Bryan Hextall, who topped the league in goals with 24 in 48 games, and his linemates Phil Watson and Lynn Patrick (Lester's son). Standing guard in net was Vezina Trophy winner Davey Kerr. During the regular season, the Rangers finished in second spot, three points back of the Boston Bruins.

New York required six games to dispose of the Bruins in the semi-final, then met the Maple Leafs in a hard-fought final series that lasted another six. Three matches, including the final game in Toronto, extended into overtime, and each time New York came out on top.

Hextall scored the Cup-winner at 2:07 of extra play after the Rangers had fought back from a 2–0 deficit to tie the score. A left-handed-shooting right winger, Hextall took a pass from Watson just inside the Toronto blue line and rifled a high backhand shot past Leaf goaltender Turk Broda.

It is said that during the post-game celebration at a Toronto hotel, Hextall and his teammates reverently passed around the Cup, each taking a lingering sip from the grail's brim. The next drink would be a long time coming.

During the post-game celebration, Hextall and his teammates reverently passed around the Cup, each taking a lingering sip.

Bryan Hextall, the hero of the final game, accepts the congratulations of Ranger coach Frank Boucher (bottom right). The Blueshirts finished fourth the next season and first in 1942, then made the playoffs only twice in the next 13 years.

Bep Guidolin debuts at sweet sixteen

"I absolutely froze. I had goose bumps and I was scared."

- Bep Guidolin

With more than 80 former NHL regulars away in the armed forces during the wartime season of 1942–43, general managers cast desperately about for replacements — no matter how young or inexperienced.

"Geez, sir, do you know I'm only 16?" Armand "Bep" Guidolin asked the Boston Bruins scout who invited him to the team's training camp that fall.

A left winger for the junior Oshawa Generals, Guidolin was a top prospect with dazzling speed and a deft touch around the net. As talented as he was, under normal conditions he could have expected to play at least two more seasons in junior and then apprentice in the minors for a year or two more before earning a spot on the varsity squad.

But those weren't normal times, and on November 12, 1942, Guidolin, a month shy of his 17th birthday, became the youngest player in NHL history when he made his debut with the Bruins at Toronto's Maple Leaf Gardens.

Guidolin later remembered how nervous he had been when he stepped onto the ice.

"I froze," he said. "I absolutely froze. I had goose bumps and I was scared. I fell a couple of times on my first two shifts and then I managed to settle down."

At first such Bruin veterans as Busher Jackson, Bill Cowley and Dit Clapper treated Guidolin with disdain.

"But I could skate by all of them," he said. "Only trouble was, I didn't always know where I was going."

Two nights after his debut Guidolin scored a pair of goals against Chicago. He went on to a solid nine-year career with Boston, Detroit and Chicago, and later coached in the NHL with the Bruins and the expansion Kansas City Scouts.

Guidolin added that he didn't agree with the current minimum-age restriction of 18.

"I'm proud of the fact that I'm the youngest ever to play in the NHL," he said. "If a kid is good enough at 16 or 17, let him play."

Guidolin (left) wasn't the only youth rushed into action due to the wartime player shortage. Seventeen-year-old goalie Harry Lumley saw duty with Detroit the next season.

The painful triumph of Frank "Ulcers" McCool

April 22, 1945

Late in the seventh game of a tension-filled Cup final, the stomach troubles that had earned Toronto's rookie goaltender Frank McCool the nickname "Ulcers" caused him to double over in pain. So great was his distress that the referee gave McCool permission to retreat to the Leaf dressing room at the Detroit Olympia for a short rest and a soothing drink of stomach medicine.

Few players have ever suffered so much for their craft. After taking over the Toronto netminding chores at the start of the season for Turk Broda, who was away in the military, the 26-year-old played brilliantly despite being in almost constant pain. McCool led the league in shutouts, and would win the Calder Trophy as the top rookie.

Although his nerves were frayed to the breaking point as the Maple Leafs progressed in the playoffs, McCool played a leading role as Toronto eliminated the Canadiens in the opening round. Then he astonished the hockey world by shutting out Detroit 1–0, 2–0 and 1–0 in the first three games of the finals. Although he was on the verge of collapse by the end of every game, few goalies had ever played better.

But the Wings managed to fight back from the abyss, winning three straight to force a deciding seventh match in Detroit.

By this point McCool's inflamed stomach had reached its limit. With the score tied 1–1 midway through the third period, he retired to the Leaf dressing room to spend ten minutes sipping his medicine and summoning his strength before forcing himself back on to the ice.

Shortly after his return, the Leafs Babe Pratt slid the puck under Detroit netminder Harry Lumley to put the Leafs ahead 2–1.

Now it was up to McCool to hold the lead. With the desperate Wings pressing the attack, he kicked back half a dozen excellent chances before the buzzer finally sounded.

The night belonged to Toronto's heroic goaltender, whose stay in the spotlight would be all too brief. With Broda back from the war, Frank "Ulcers" McCool was gone from the NHL by the end of the next season.

Although he was on the verge of collapse, few goalies had ever played better.

In this action shot from the 1945 season, Frank McCool guards the Toronto cage as Leaf defenceman Wally Stanowski attempts to tie up Ranger Ab DeMarco. New York's Hank Goldup looms in the background.

Syl Apps retires a contented Leaf

His only remaining ambition was to attain the 200-goal plateau, a feat accomplished by only one other Leaf, Charlie Conacher.

Toronto captain Syl Apps shocked fans and teammates late in the season when he announced his intention to retire after the playoffs. It was true that at age 33 Apps had lost a step, but he was still one of the classiest centres in the league, and he was enjoying his most productive season ever.

Considered the team's spiritual leader, Apps had won the Calder Trophy as the league's top rookie in 1937, and been awarded the Lady Byng for gentlemanly play in 1942. As captain, he had led the Leafs to Stanley Cup victories in 1942 and again in 1947.

Apps said he was quitting to spend more time with his family. His only remaining career ambition was to attain the 200-goal plateau, a feat that had been accomplished by only one other Leaf, Charlie Conacher, who scored exactly 200.

He was still two short as Toronto travelled to Detroit for the final match of the regular season. Early in the second period, Apps narrowed the gap when he scored from a scramble in front of Red Wing goaltender Harry Lumley.

His coveted 200th came just 3:40 later. Teammate Harry Watson raced in and had Lumley beaten, but at the last moment he passed the puck to his captain, who slammed it home.

A laughing Apps dived into the net to retrieve the puck, then skated back to the Leaf bench where he was mobbed by his teammates as the Detroit fans graciously offered a long ovation. Apps scored another in the third period to complete the hat-trick and pass Conacher to become Toronto's all-time leading goal scorer. It was his 26th goal of the season, the highest total of his career.

In the dressing room after the Leafs 5–2 victory, there was considerable comment about how generous it was of Harry Watson to set up Apps for his 200th goal when he could have so easily scored himself.

"It was nice of him all right," laughed Apps, whose final act as captain would be to lead the Leafs to their second consecutive Stanley Cup. "But you should have heard the yelling I was doing at him to pass it!"

Apps was one of the most accomplished and popular players ever to skate for the Maple Leafs. "He's been my meal ticket for 10 years," said Toronto goalie Turk Broda. "When things look rugged, Hap [coach Hap Day] drops him over the boards and the situation improves instantly."

Famous Kraut Line lives again in Boston

Milt Schmidt responded with a remarkable performance, figuring in all the scoring.

As the three members of the famous Kraut Line stood misty-eyed in the glare of the spotlight, ushers paraded across the ice carrying china sets, movie cameras, juke boxes, golf clubs and dozens of other gifts from the Boston fans. When the procession finally ended, Milt Schmidt told the capacity crowd of 13,909: "Through the years you've already given me the best present of all — your friendship and support." Added Woody Dumart: "It's been a wonderful pleasure to play all my hockey here in Boston."

Schmidt and Dumart were being honoured for years of brilliant service in the Boston cause. Making the evening even more memorable was the appearance in uniform of Bobby Bauer, who had temporarily ended his five-year retirement to skate alongside his former linemates one last time.

Centre Schmidt and left and right wingers Dumart and Bauer first played together as juniors in their home town of Kitchener, Ontario, which had a large German population. By 1937 they were combining their talents for the Bruins on what became one of the most colourful and explosive forward units in history.

Milt Schmidt responded to the cheers of the gala audience with a remarkable performance, figuring in all the scoring as Boston shut out the Chicago Black Hawks 4–0.

Years later Schmidt said that the highlight of his career came in the second period when he scored his 200th goal, with assists to Bauer and Dumart. Chicago netminder Harry Lumley directed a shot by Bauer into the corner, but Dumart gathered the loose puck and relayed it back to Schmidt, who blasted it past Lumley from about ten feet out.

In the third period, Bauer brought the fans back to their feet when he notched his first goal since 1947. After taking a lead pass from Schmidt, he stick-handled around Lumley and back-handed the puck into the corner of the net.

Although he tired easily, Bauer had looked so good it was suggested that he stay with the team. He declined, citing business duties back home in Kitchener.

"It was a wonderful experience, though," he said of the Kraut Line's reunion. "I'll never forget it."

Neither would the Boston fans.

Milt Schmidt (bottom left) scored 229 goals in 16 seasons, all with Boston. "Schmidt was the fastest playmaker of all time," marvelled Bruin boss Art Ross. "No player ever skated at full tilt the way he did and was still able to make the play." The famous Kraut Line (top left) of Bobby Bauer, Schmidt and Woody Dumart led the Bruins to four straight league titles and two Stanley Cups between 1938 and 1941.

Richard tops Stewart's all-time scoring mark

November 8, 1952

Even after having savoured so many great moments, Maurice "Rocket" Richard was in awe of his newest accomplishment.

Canadiens coach Dick Irvin said Richard was white as a sheet when he skated over with the puck he'd used to break Nels Stewart's all-time scoring mark of 324 goals. "I was afraid he was going to pass out right in front of the bench."

Richard's historic score came while the crowd of 14,562 at the Montreal Forum was still in an uproar over another milestone achievement: Elmer Lach's 200th career goal. Just 50 seconds after setting up his linemate's second-period score, Richard took a pass from Butch Bouchard and broke in on Chicago Black Hawks goaltender Al Rollins.

He fired a backhander from about 20 feet out. Rollins got a piece of it, but the puck just managed to trickle through into the net. "A great shout went up, flash bulbs went off, and play was halted while the Rocket recovered the puck and took it over to Dick Irvin on the Canadiens bench," recounted the Montreal *Gazette*. "His teammates pounded him gleefully on the back."

Within minutes, Richard had received a wire from Nels Stewart, the old Montreal Maroons star whose record he had eclipsed. "Congratulations on breaking the record," it read. "Hope you will hold it for many seasons. Best of luck to you, Frank Selke [Montreal GM], Dick Irvin and the rest of the boys through the season."

Richard's nerves had settled by the time he met reporters after the game, which the Canadiens won 6–4. "It was the greatest thrill of my hockey career," the hockey legend pronounced, "but I'm glad it's over. Too much pressure."

Typically, Richard tried to deflect some of the spotlight onto Lach, his longtime centre and close friend. "I'm glad Elmer got his 200th goal," the Rocket said. "It's been an honour and a privilege to play with him all these years."

Nels Stewart (above), the Montreal Maroons star whose record Richard eclipsed. In the photo at top right, a typically determined Rocket breaks in on Toronto netminder Harry Lumley.

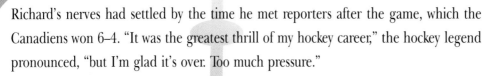

"A great shout went up, flash bulbs went off, and play was halted while the Rocket recovered the puck."

- Montreal Gazette

Punch Imlach's over-the-hill gang

May 2, 1967

"Some of you have been with me for nine years," Toronto coach and general manager Punch Imlach told his troops before the sixth game of their Cup final with the Montreal Canadiens. "It has been said that I stuck with the old men so long we couldn't possibly win the Stanley Cup. For some of you it's a farewell. Go out there and put that puck down their throats!"

The confrontation between hockey's arch-rivals became a cherished memory of Canada's 1967 Centennial celebrations. No matter what their loyalties, fans across the country took comfort in knowing that the Cup would stay on Canadian soil.

It was true that Imlach demonstrated a fierce loyalty to the veterans (seven of whom were age 36 or older) who had led Toronto to three Cups in the past five years. But most observers believed too few changes had been made, and were amazed that the aging Leafs had come this far.

Toronto defeated first-place Chicago in six games in the opening round of the playoffs, and had pushed Montreal, two-time defending Cup champions, to the brink of elimination, leading 3–2 in the series.

Much of the credit for the Leafs success was given to the veteran goaltending tandem of Terry Sawchuk and Johnny Bower. Sawchuk, in particular, had been outstanding, playing as brilliantly as he had when he first broke in with Detroit in the early 1950s.

In the sixth game, Sawchuk turned back 46 shots. With a minute left to play, the Leafs led 2–1. Canadiens coach Toe Blake removed goalie Gump Worsley for an extra attacker. Imlach countered by sending out his most grizzled veterans to protect the lead — Tim Horton, Red Kelly, Allan Stanley and George Armstrong. Stanley, 41, muscled Jean Beliveau off the puck on the draw. Kelly stole it and passed to Armstrong, who took aim and put an insurance goal in the Canadiens net.

"A lot of wise guys said this team wasn't good enough," Imlach said afterwards. "Some of them may retire and others may be lost in the expansion draft. But now they're going out as champs, and that's the way it should be."

Captain George Armstrong, who scored the final goal in the Toronto triumph, carries the Cup during the victory celebration at Maple Leaf Gardens.

*"Go out there
and put that
puck down
their throats!"*

- Punch Imlach

Espo and the trade that built the Bruins

May 15, 1967

One night, when Phil Esposito scored three goals against his former Chicago teammates, Bobby Hull is said to have skated back to the Hawk bench and yelled bitterly at coach Billy Reay: "Well, I hope that you're satisfied with your deal."

Infamous in hockey history as *The Trade*, the transaction that sent centres Esposito and Fred Stanfield as well as winger Ken Hodge to Boston propelled the Bruins to two Stanley Cup championships in the years ahead and might have cost the Hawks at least that many. In return, Chicago received Pit Martin, a slightly built winger who had several productive seasons but was never a standout; young defenceman Gilles Marotte, who failed to live up to his considerable potential; and goaltender Jack Norris, who played only ten games for the Hawks.

Although at age 25 Esposito hadn't yet attained stardom, many were shocked that Chicago would let such an obviously gifted playmaker get away. He had joined the Hawks in 1963 and played centre on a line with Bobby Hull starting the next year. In three full seasons, Esposito scored 23, 27 and 21 goals, and helped Hull to consecutive campaigns of 54 and 52 goals.

But Chicago general manager Tommy Ivan and coach Reay found Esposito wanting. They criticized his choppy skating style and, mostly, his lack of point production when it counted most, in the playoffs.

With Esposito, Hodge and Stanfield leading the way up front, Boston rose from the basement to third place the first year after the trade and second the next, while the Hawks dropped from first place to fourth and then fell into the cellar.

The trio wasted no time in showing their former employers the magnitude of their mistake. In their first match against the Hawks, they all scored or assisted on at least one goal in a 7–1 shellacking.

"The three of us received a great deal of satisfaction from that game," said Esposito, who soon answered his critics by setting scoring records and becoming renowned as an inspirational team leader. "It's always nice to score against the team that traded you."

Approached by reporters, Tommy Ivan and Billy Reay refused to comment.

Phil Esposito fights off Toronto defenceman Allan Stanley in the photo above. Pit Martin, at right, was coming off a 20-goal season with the Bruins when he was dealt to Chicago. He went on to score 324 goals in a 17-year career; Esposito notched 717 in 18 seasons.

Many were shocked that Chicago let Esposito get away.

Toe Blake goes out a champion

May 11, 1968

The raucous joking, back slapping and spraying of champagne suddenly stopped. In the midst of celebrating their Stanley Cup triumph over St. Louis, the Montreal Canadiens heard the news that their coach Toe Blake had called it quits.

"This is my last year," announced Blake. "I'd like to coach the Canadiens for a hundred years, but the tension is too much. On the days of some games this year, I was almost not human."

At first his players refused to accept what they were hearing. "I'll believe it when they sign a new coach," said veteran centre Ralph Backstrom. "The Bear says this every spring. He's just fed up with hockey like the rest of us."

But at age 55 Blake had nothing left to prove, and he was serious about having had enough. All told, Blake had spent 26 years with the Canadiens as a player and a coach. He'd won the scoring championship as well as the Hart Trophy as the league's most valuable player in 1938–39. Later on he was the left winger on the famous Punch line with centre Elmer Lach and Maurice "Rocket" Richard.

After taking over as coach from Dick Irvin prior to the start of the 1955–56 season, Blake had guided the Canadiens to nine league titles and eight Stanley Cups, including a record five in a row between 1956 and 1960. To this day, no coach has matched his record for Stanley Cup championships.

Still in shock, his players talked about how much he'd meant to them, and how they'd miss him.

"I never met a man with such an intense desire to win," said John Ferguson. "If I had to single out the greatest of his qualities that would be it. His desire — it affects all of us."

"He made me realize what it's like to work hard and how hard work pays off," added Yvan Cournoyer. Gilles Tremblay talked about his coach's brilliant record and predicted that the best measure of his coaching abilities was yet to come.

"We'll know how good he was when he's gone," Tremblay said in the gloom of the champions' dressing room.

"He just about came apart at the seams after our last game," said Canadiens goalie Gump Worsley when Toe Blake (seen here behind the Montreal bench) called it quits. "His nerves must be all shot. I'd hate to be the guy to replace him. How do you improve on excellence?"

"He made me realize how hard work pays off."

- Yvan Cournoyer

Ken Dryden makes his case

May 18, 1971

Montreal's rookie netminder Ken Dryden astonished onlookers with his superlative play throughout the playoffs, but his shining moment undeniably came with the Stanley Cup on the line in the seventh game of the final against Chicago.

The unflappable 23-year-old made 31 stops. Tony Esposito in the Hawk net made 22. In the third period, with the Canadiens nursing a 3–2 lead, Dryden robbed Stan Mikita, Bobby Hull, Eric Nesterenko and Jim Pappin from point-blank range.

What made Dryden's performance throughout the playoffs all the more remarkable was that it was so totally unexpected. He had played in just six regular season games after being called up from the Montreal Voyageurs of the American Hockey League. As the Canadiens entered the playoffs, analysts agreed that goaltending was their one glaring weakness.

Dryden's save on Pappin in the dying moments of the last game clinched the victory for Montreal and had the 21,000 frustrated fans jammed into Chicago Stadium rubbing their eyes in disbelief.

Hawk defenceman Keith Magnuson took a shot from the right boards that Dryden kicked out. Pappin picked up the rebound and, from about three feet out, snapped a shot that Dryden somehow got his leg in front of.

"I saw Magnuson shoot, and knew Pappin would be close," the 6'4" goaltender told reporters minutes later as the Canadiens celebrated their 17th Cup win. "It was instinct, I guess, that I shoved out my leg to make the save."

Dryden, a law student at McGill University in the off season, was the first rookie goaltender to backstop a club to the Stanley Cup since Frank "Ulcers" McCool did it with Toronto in 1945. And he became the first rookie to win the Conn Smythe Trophy as the most valuable player in the playoffs.

After presenting Canadiens captain Jean Beliveau with the Cup, NHL president Clarence Campbell called the post-season the most exciting he'd seen since his association with the league began in 1936. "As for the hero of this year's playoffs?" he said. "Undoubtedly Ken Dryden."

Dryden robbed Mikita, Hull and Pappin from point-blank range.

Ken Dryden is seen here in two characteristic poses. At right, he leans forward, using his stick as a support during a break in the action; above, he assumes the panther-like crouch that was all business.

Team Canada meets the amazing Mr. Tretiak

September 6, 1972

> *"Tretiak is as good as I've seen anywhere."*
>
> *- Paul Henderson*

Watching the Soviets practice before the start of their historic summit series, some members of Team Canada actually expressed concern for the safety of slim goalie Vladislav Tretiak. Thinking of the lethal slapshots of Dennis Hull and other members of the Canadian squad, defenceman Brad Park shook his head and said, "Do they really know what they're letting their goaltender in for?"

Like the rest of his teammates, Tretiak was considered a pushover by his haughty opponents. An advance scouting report, which was soon to become the butt of bitter jokes, described the 20-year-old to be of "Junior B calibre."

By the end of the third game of the series in Winnipeg on September 6, the Soviets had not only proved themselves to be at least the equal of Team Canada in every regard, but Tretiak was being called one of the best goaltenders on the planet.

"I blew it, I blew the chance to win," lamented Canadian left winger Paul Henderson after the two teams had fought to a thrilling 4–4 tie. "I had three terrific chances but he made the saves."

Henderson, who managed to put one goal past Tretiak, was foiled at point-blank range early in the third period when the Soviet snaked out his hand and made what reporters described as "the save of the tournament." He made another equally spectacular stop on Brad Park, and about a dozen more that could easily have been goals. For the second consecutive game, Tretiak was named his team's outstanding player.

Tretiak told the Canadian press that he had modelled his goaltending style on that of his mentor, Victor Konavalenko, who for years had been the top goaltender in his country. He also said that he'd received helpful tutoring from the great Jacques Plante both on an earlier trip to Canada and prior to the start of the series.

Canadians fervently wished that Plante had kept his secrets to himself. After three games, each side had one win as well as the tie in Winnipeg.

"Tretiak is as good as I've seen anywhere," said an exasperated Paul Henderson. Fortunately for Team Canada, he would have considerably better luck against the sensational young goaltender in Moscow.

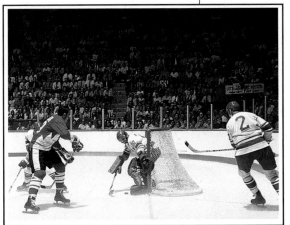

The young goalie told reporters that he honed his remarkable reflexes by taking two rubber balls and continuously bouncing them against the wall. In the photo above, Tretiak faces down Team Canada's Frank Mahovlich.

Montreal hosts a New Year's Eve rebirth

December 31, 1975

The Canadiens outshot the Soviets 38–13 and outplayed them throughout the game.

By the mid-1970s many longtime fans had come to fear that the game they loved was in danger of being destroyed by too-rapid expansion and the popularity of what was called "goon hockey." Some believed that the only solution was to adopt the supposedly more skillful, wide-open style of play preferred by the Soviets.

Then, in an exhibition match on New Year's Eve, the Montreal Canadiens resurrected North American hockey's proud heritage by completely dominating Central Red Army in a 3–3 tie. Those in attendance at the Montreal Forum and the millions more who watched on television agreed that it was one of the most thrilling demonstrations of team play ever seen.

The roster of the Soviet Union's top club team included most of that country's best players, including Vladislav Tretiak, Valeri Kharlamov and Boris Mikhailov. Yet the Canadiens, who would go on to win the first of four consecutive Stanley Cups, outshot the touring Soviets 38–13 and outplayed them throughout the game. If not for the spectacular goaltending of old nemesis Tretiak, the Canadiens might have won by a margin of five or six goals.

Steve Shutt and Yvon Lambert scored to put Montreal ahead 2–0 in the first period, a lead that stood until the second frame when a weak shot by Mikhailov beat an unusually tentative Ken Dryden in the Montreal net. Yvan Cournoyer's power play goal soon restored the Canadiens two-goal advantage.

In the third period, Kharlamov beat Dryden cleanly for Red Army's second goal. But the shot by Boris Aleksandrov that evened the score at 3–3 was another that should have been stopped.

Montreal's forechecking was so consistently devastating that Red Army was unable to execute the precision passing patterns for which Soviet teams were famous. The Canadiens defence was almost impenetrable.

Scotty Bowman said afterwards that he had never been prouder of his team — or more convinced that North American-style hockey was again on the right track. "I don't think we have to take a back seat to anybody," Bowman said. "They were outclassed for 60 minutes except for the goaltending. I really don't think our hockey is so bad."

Pete Mahovlich, Vladislav Tretiak and Yvan Cournoyer (left) were named the three stars of one of the most exciting games ever played. If not for the spectacular performance of Soviet netminder Tretiak (above), Montreal might have won by five or six goals.

Howe to Howe to Howe

March 12, 1980

It was the first time that a father-and-son combo had appeared in the same NHL lineup.

Although he hadn't officially announced his impending retirement, 19,041 old friends turned out for what was likely to be Gordie Howe's last appearance at the Detroit Olympia as an active player. When the 51-year-old legend skated out to take the opening faceoff, flanked on the wings by his sons Mark and Marty, the crowd stood and lustily cheered their thanks for many lifetimes of memories.

Now wearing the uniform of the Hartford Whalers, the former Red Wing great had realized his final career ambition three days before when Marty was called up from the minors to join him and youngest son Mark for a game against Boston. Although the trio of Howes had played together for six years in the World Hockey Association, it was the first time that a father-and-son combo had appeared in the same NHL lineup.

Gordie suited up for all 80 games and scored 15 goals for the Whalers, who had joined the NHL before the start of the season along with three other former WHA teams. But even pro hockey's only playing grandfather couldn't go on forever. For weeks he had been teasing the press about an impending announcement.

Hartford coach Don Blackburn made the Howes his starting forward line, even though both sons were ordinarily defencemen.

"Why not?" said Blackburn. "The kids lived here all their lives and Gordie half his life. Gordie's deserving of every accolade and it gave the kids a chance to enjoy something very meaningful."

At the conclusion of a 4–4 tie, the press tried to prod Howe into announcing his retirement.

"The doctor told me not to play this year and I ignored him," said No. 9, whose 52nd birthday was only 19 days away. "I'll probably ignore him next year, too."

But Howe was just having his fun. After scoring the 1,071st and final goal of his 32-year NHL and WHA career in the playoffs, the legend known as Mr. Hockey finally, and this time permanently, called it quits.

With Gordie taking the opening faceoff, the Howes line up at the Olympia (left). Mark, Gordie and Marty pose for photographers before the game (above).

New York Islanders give birth to a dynasty

The Islanders had too much talent and were too well coached to be denied any longer.

Butch Goring and Denis Potvin, hoisting the Cup, celebrate the first of four consecutive Stanley Cups the Islanders would win (left). Bob Nystrom beats Philadelphia goalie Pete Peeters for the Cup-winning goal (above).

After so many earlier disappointments, the New York Islanders felt more relieved than elated at finally having won the Stanley Cup. "We heard 'hapless' to describe us in our early days in this league and 'choke' in the past few seasons," said coach Al Arbour. "Thank heavens we won't hear those words now."

The Islanders got pinned with the 'hapless' tag when they won just 12 and 19 games the first two seasons after they came into the league in 1972–73. The 'choke' label stuck when a run of excellent regular-season finishes was followed by upset defeats in the playoffs.

But the Islanders had too much talent and were too well coached to be denied any longer. Denis Potvin was the league's top rearguard, centre Bryan Trottier set a new post-season point record of 29 and was awarded the Conn Smythe Trophy, and sniper Mike Bossy was the leading scorer in the finals.

To a man, the Islanders lavished praise on coach Arbour, believing that more than anyone he deserved credit for the Cup win. Arbour felt that the Islanders had worn themselves out the season before when they finished first overall during the regular schedule. So this season he pointed their efforts towards the playoffs, unconcerned that four clubs finished with more points.

The Islanders defeated Los Angeles, Boston and Buffalo before meeting Philadelphia in a gruelling six-game final. Renowned as the Broad Street Bullies, the Flyers tried the usual intimidation tactics on their more talented opponents, only to be repeatedly victimized by the Islander power play.

The final game was tied 4–4 when winger Bob Nystrom swept a pass from John Tonelli under Flyer netminder Pete Peeters for the Cup-winner at 7:11 of overtime. The euphoric crowd at Nassau Country Coliseum immediately broke into a chorus of Queen's "We Are The Champions."

"The real history of this team starts now," said Islander Bob Bourne amidst the revelry of the dressing room. "Forget all that other stuff."

The new label was "dynasty."

Reluctant Bowman hockey's winningest coach

February 18, 1985

Although he was credited with having broken Dick Irvin's record of 690 career coaching victories back on December 19, 1984, when his Buffalo Sabres defeated Chicago 6–3, Scotty Bowman, ever the perfectionist, begged to differ with the official NHL game count.

"I felt I shouldn't get credit for winning games when one of my assistants was actually coaching the club," he said. "The NHL position is that what counts is who was the head coach, whether or not he was actually present. I'd have tried to block this thing tonight if I didn't really have the right total. But I'm well over now."

Bowman was referring to the gala ceremony held to honour his achievement prior to that night's match against the Edmonton Oilers at the Buffalo Auditorium. Joining in the tribute were the 51-year-old coach's family, NHL president John Ziegler, and several of his former players, including Guy Lafleur.

A giant plaque, with gold pucks shaped to form 691, was presented to Bowman at centre ice as the sellout crowd stood for a two-minute ovation.

"A night like this is something that only happens once in your career," Bowman had said before the festivities got started. Famous for figuring all the angles, the coach admitted to being a little worried. "These emotional situations often turn out to be a bad thing. I mean, we went into Montreal on Guy Lafleur Night last Saturday and beat the Canadiens. You know what I mean?"

Bowman began his NHL coaching career with St. Louis in 1967–68, and then joined Montreal in 1971. After leading the Canadiens to five Stanley Cups, he moved on to Buffalo as general manager and coach in June 1979.

Guy Lafleur stepped forward during the ceremony and called Bowman the best coach he'd ever played for. "He was so sharp behind the bench that I never saw anyone outcoach him."

Bowman handled a ceremonial faceoff to wrap up the proceedings. Then the fears of the winningest coach in the game were realized as his Sabres lost 6–4 to the Oilers. The Bowman victory march now *officially* stood at 707 and counting.

"I never saw anyone outcoach him."

- Guy Lafleur

Scotty Bowman turned to coaching as a teenager after a fractured skull ended his promising playing career. Above, Bowman says his thanks to the crowd of 16,433 in Buffalo that turned out to honour him.

Gretzky bids a tearful farewell to Edmonton

August 9, 1988

Hockey's greatest star tried to express his feelings about leaving the team he had led to four Stanley Cups, and about the city that had taken him to its heart. "There comes a time when…" Tears prevented Wayne Gretzky from going on. He turned away from the bank of microphones to collect himself.

"You gotta be nuts to trade Wayne Gretzky!" raged a caller to an Edmonton radio station when the deal with the Los Angeles Kings was announced. That seemed to be the sentiments of shocked fans right across Canada. In Ottawa, a member of Parliament called on the government to block the trade, saying Wayne Gretzky was "as much a national symbol as the beaver."

"I felt it was a good career move…and it was also an opportunity to help not only this team, but the game of hockey," Gretzky told the reporters in Edmonton after he had regained his composure. He said he had requested the trade so that he and his bride, L.A.-based actress Janet Jones, could spend as much time as possible together.

The deal, described as one of the biggest in the history of sport, sent Gretzky to L.A. along with forward Mike Krushelnyski and enforcer Marty McSorley. In return, the Oilers received high-scoring centre Jimmy Carson, left winger Martin Gelinas, and the Kings first-round picks in 1989, 1991 and 1992.

Kings owner Bruce McNall also revealed that he had made a cash payment "in excess of $10 million (U.S.)" to the Oilers.

Many NHL executives agreed with Gretzky that the trade would benefit hockey. His presence in Los Angeles would help to sell the game throughout the American market.

A second press conference was held that night in Los Angeles. "This morning was very difficult for me," Gretzky said. "Tonight, it's all upbeat. I'm very excited to be here."

At least one of Gretzky's new teammates had difficulty describing how it felt to suddenly have the famous number 99 as a teammate.

"It's, uh, pretty, uh, very, very blockbustering — if that's a word," managed Kings right winger Jimmy Fox. "This is unbelievable. He's the best player in the world."

> ## "You gotta be nuts to trade Wayne Gretzky!"
>
> ## - Radio caller

A tearful Gretzky at the press conference in Edmonton to announce his trade. He had set an amazing 43 league scoring records while with the Oilers, including most goals (92), assists (163) and points (215) in a season.

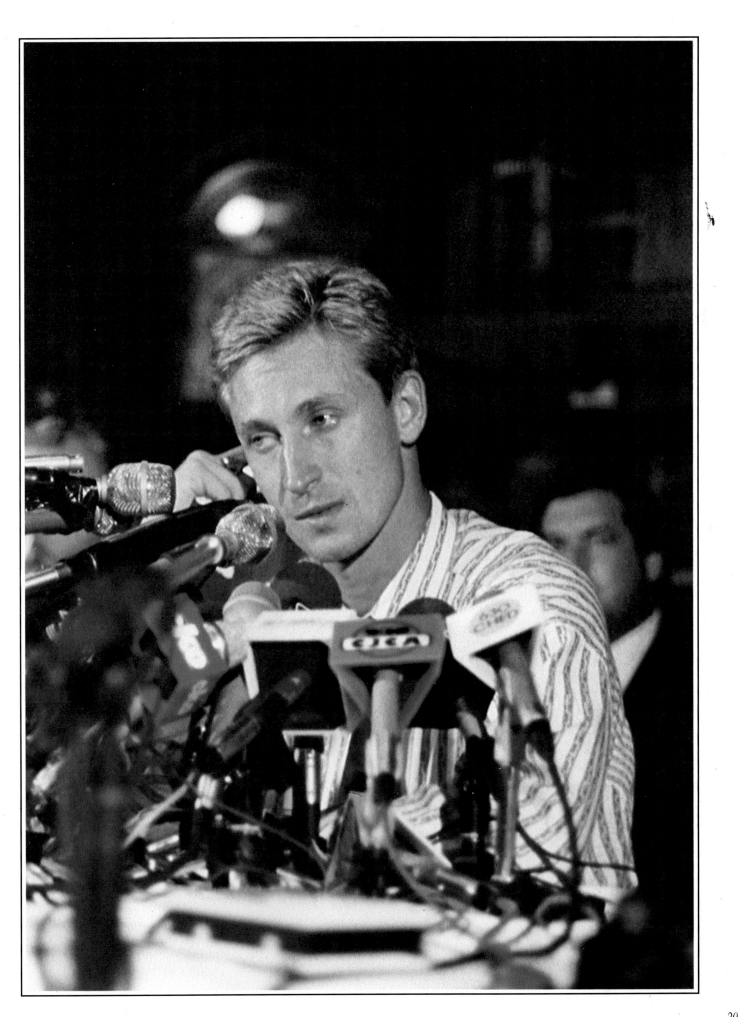

Lanny McDonald's Cinderella finish

May 25, 1989

"It's a hell of a way to write the final chapter."

- Lanny McDonald

After the 1,128th and final game of his career, McDonald finally held the Stanley Cup aloft. "It's the most peaceful feeling I've ever experienced in hockey," he said.

After waiting 16 seasons for just this moment, Calgary's Lanny McDonald finally held the Stanley Cup aloft in triumph. "There's no weight to it," the red-haired winger with the Yosemite Sam moustache said in surprise. "It's the nicest feeling in the world."

Though he'd played only sparingly, McDonald was the popular hero of the six-game victory over the Montreal Canadiens. Back home in Calgary, many in the crowd of thousands that swarmed the downtown streets to celebrate the Flames first championship pasted on huge red moustaches in his honour.

For McDonald, the victory was the culmination of a dream as well as a storybook ending to an illustrious career. At the start of the season he announced that this would be his final campaign. On March 7 McDonald scored his 1,000th career point, and two weeks later he netted his 500th goal.

The Flames 36-year-old co-captain (an honour he shared with Joe Peplinski) scored just 11 goals during the regular schedule and often sat on the bench as Calgary battled its way past Vancouver, Los Angeles and Chicago to reach the Cup final.

McDonald hadn't even suited up for the previous three games as the Flames took a 3–2 series lead. Then, 30 minutes before the start of game six at the Montreal Forum, coach Terry Crisp told him he'd be playing.

"I was ecstatic," McDonald said. "But I didn't just want to be out there, I wanted to be part of the reason we won."

McDonald responded with his first goal of the playoffs, which gave the Flames a 2–1 lead early in the second period. After taking a pass from Joe Nieuwendyk, McDonald skated in and beat Canadiens goaltender Patrick Roy with a rising wrist shot. It was the 44th goal of his 117-game playoff career. The Flames went on to a 4–2 Cup-clinching victory.

Between sips of champagne, McDonald talked about the "Cinderella finish" to his career.

"I don't know if it's a storybook ending or not," he said, thoughtfully stroking his luxuriant moustache. "But it's a hell of a way to write the final chapter."

205

Eric Lindros breaks the Philly bank

"I'm pumped, I'm jacked to the nines," enthused teenage sensation Eric Lindros shortly before signing a multi-year deal with the Philadelphia Flyers that would make him one of the highest paid players in the game. "I'll give the effort and earn the money — there's no doubt about that."

The most ballyhooed rookie since Mario Lemieux, Lindros, 19, had made headlines for the past year with his stubborn refusal to sign with the Quebec Nordiques, the team that originally drafted him. Lindros said that he feared playing in the small francophone market would restrict his off-ice endorsements. He also said he didn't want to live in a province that was threatening to separate from the rest of Canada.

Many Quebecers reacted with stunned indignation to Lindros' comments. Nationalists decried his attitude as yet another slap in the face by English Canada.

After a year in which Lindros occupied his time by playing brilliantly for Canada in the Canada Cup and competing with the Canadian team in the Winter Olympics, the Nordiques finally traded his rights — to two teams on the same day. Both Philadelphia and the New York Rangers claimed that they had finalized deals for Lindros with Quebec. The NHL was forced to call in an arbitor, who ruled in favour of the Flyers.

In return for the 6'5", 225-pound centre, Philadelphia shipped the Nordiques five frontline players, including goalie Ron Hextall and centre Mike Ricci, a first-round draft pick in 1993, and US$15 million. Then they agreed to pay Lindros an estimated $15 million to $18 million over six years, including a signing bonus. Only Wayne Gretzky was making more than Lindros's annual stipend of about $2.5 million.

There were those who felt that Philadelphia had given up too much, even for a potential franchise player like Lindros. But Flyers chairman Ed Snider had no such doubts.

"The contract we made is indicative of how important we feel Eric is to our organization," he said, adding that he felt confident Lindros would help fill the 21,000-seat arena he intended to build. "Our goal is to win the Stanley Cup. Eric is the perfect fit for what we hope to accomplish."

> *"I'll give the effort and earn the money — there's no doubt about that."*
>
> *- Eric Lindros*

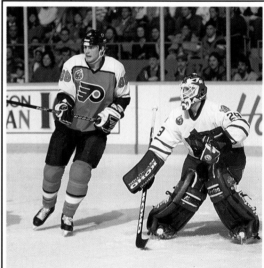

Even before he played a game in the NHL, many analysts were calling Lindros one of the best players in hockey. Above, he takes position in front of Toronto goaltender Felix Potvin.

Finnish Flash shatters Bossy's rookie record

March 2, 1993

> *"I just hope I can keep this record for the next 15 years."*
>
> *- Teemu Selanne*

"Teemu-mania" was how Winnipeg newspapers described the excitement surrounding Jets rookie Teemu Selanne's assault on the NHL record book. No first-year player had ever demonstrated the prolific scoring touch of the 22-year-old right winger known as the Finnish Flash.

Selanne required just 64 games to surpass Mike Bossy's rookie scoring mark of 53, which had stood for 15 years. The record-breaker came in Winnipeg against the Quebec Nordiques when Selanne chased down a long flip pass from Tie Domi and chopped the puck past goaltender Stephane Fiset for his third goal of the night.

After Selanne scored, he twirled around and threw his right glove high in the air, then raised his stick and pretended to shoot the glove down. It was a ritual Selanne had performed after big goals in his native Finland and had been saving until this moment for his new fans.

The near-capacity crowd of 14,397 loved it, applauding wildly for more than five minutes as Selanne accepted the congratulations of his teammates and was presented with a silver-plated stick by Jets president Barry Shenkarow.

"I just hope I can keep this record for the next 15 years," said Selanne, who had also broken the Jets all-time single season goal-scoring mark of 53 held by Dale Hawerchuk. "Getting that first goal tonight gave me so much confidence. But really, I wasn't thinking too much about it before the game."

Selanne went on to score 76 goals and 132 points, then received 36 of 50 first-place votes in being named to the first all-star team. To no one's surprise, he also took home the Calder Trophy as the top rookie.

The Finn even managed that with his usual flair. Selanne received 50 out of 50 first-place votes — the first unanimous decision in the history of the award.

Jets president Barry Shenkarow presents Selanne with a silver-plated stick to commemorate the occasion (above). "It's a cliche but all records are set to be broken," said Mike Bossy. "I'm just glad it was broken by a player of his calibre."

ON THE MAKING OF THIS BOOK

Jacket and interior designed by Clifford T. Amemori,
with special thanks to V. John Lee, mentor and friend.

Photo selection by Brian Kendall and Clifford T. Amemori

Edited by Greg Ioannou, Colborne Communication Centre

Production direction by Dianne Craig, Penguin Books

Printed and bound by New Interlitho Italia S.p.A. on acid neutral paper.

The typeface used throughout *100 Great Moments in Hockey* is New Baskerville Condensed.
Layout and typesetting have been produced on an IBM 486 with Aldus Pagemaker, Version 5.0.
The various design elements were produced with CorelDraw, Version 4.0.

PHOTO CREDITS

AP/Wide World Photos: 18 (top), 86, 135 (bottom); Harold Barkley: 20–21, 80–81; Bruce Bennett Studios: vii (bottom), 29, 32–33, 38–39, 41, 42, 48, 50, 52–53, 89, 91, 92, 94–95, 96–97, 99, 101, 103, 142 (both), 150–151, 152, 154, 156, 190, 192, 198, 201, 203, 204, 207, 208, 209; Denis Brodeur: 26–27, 30–31, 34, 35, 47, 130 (bottom), 133, 194, 195; Buffalo Sabres — Bill Wippert: 200; Michael Burns: title page, 10–11, 72–73, 128; Canapress: 28, 46, 149 (bottom); The Detroit News: 77; Globe and Mail — John Maiola: 90; Terry Hancey: 144–145; Hockey Hall of Fame: vi (both), vii (top), 4, 6, 7, 18 (bottom), 56 (top), 59 (both), 61 (both), 64, 69, 83 (bottom), 108, 109, 111 (both), 112 (bottom), 116–117, 122–123, 160, 161, 162, 163, 164, 167 (both), 168–169, 170–171, 173 (both), 174, 178, 180 (both), 182, 183 (both), 187 (bottom), 193, 199 (Goodman donation); Hockey Hall of Fame — Doug MacLellan/The Ice Age: 44, 56 (bottom), 105, 206; Hockey Hall of Fame — Imperial Oil Turofsky Collection: 9, 14, 16–17 (top), 23, 65, 66–67, 74, 78, 82–83 (top), 118 (bottom), 118–119, 188–189; Hockey Hall of Fame — Frank Prazak Collection: 13, 75, 84, 87, 130–131 (top), 134–135 (top), 136–137, 139, 141, 146–147, 184–185, 186–187 (top), 191; Heinz Kluetmeier/Sports Illustrated: 37; Dwayne LaBakas: 196, 197; La Press: 71; Raymond Lussier: 24–25; Montreal Gazette: 124–125; New York Daily News: 127 (both); Toronto Star — R. Bull: 149 (top); UPI/Bettman: 16 (bottom), 62–63, 112 (top), 115, 120, 121, 126, 177.